FULLY PRESENT

DAILY REFLECTIONS ON NONDUALITY

Rodney Stevens

Copyright © 2011 by Rodney Stevens

ISBN-13: 978-1-105-27890-7

All Rights Reserved

"You see, it's all very clear to me now. The whole thing. It's wonderful."

Col. David Bowman
2010: The Year We Made Contact

Acknowledgements

My sincere gratitude goes to Fiona Robertson for her editing, proof-reading, and sagacious suggestions. There was never a moment of hesitancy or exasperation on her part. Indeed, there was always the well-phrased nudge; "How is the December re-write going?" or "Are you ready to send me the January-June section yet?" Though I am naturally productive, she was always, somehow, ahead of even me.

Greg Banks, of BDDesign LLC, also deserves a round of hearty thanks. His self-publishing skills are as enormous as his generosity and compassion, and I simply couldn't have published this book without him.

Colleen Loehr graciously agreed to write the beautiful and clear-sighted Preface for this book. And for that, I will always be deeply grateful.

Finally, my sincere appreciation goes to John Wheeler, whose pristine clarity pointed the way.

Note: Some names have been changed to protect those persons' privacy.

The following books have been referred to in this diary:

Tao Te Ching, by Lao Tzu, translated by Stephen Mitchell (London: Francis Lincoln Limited, 1999, Chapter 45) for the January 15 entry.

Flowers Fall: A Commentary on Zen Master Dogen's Genjokoan, by Hakuun Yasutani (Boston: Shambhala, 1996, p.2) for the October 29 entry.

Table of Contents

Preface: Stopped in My Tracks 9
January 2010 12
February 37
March 45
April 56
May 60
June 67
July 78
August 92
September 102
October 111
November 115
December 124
January 2011 140

Preface: Stopped in My Tracks

When I first came across Rodney Stevens' blog a few years ago, I was immediately stopped in my tracks. Shocked into stillness by the sheer force of clarity in his words, attention moved without moving, from the finger-pointing-at-the-moon (Rodney's words) to the moon itself (ineffable presence). It was the recognition of myself, not as a personal-story-unfolding-in-time, but as something much more real, vivid, and immovable. With laser-like precision, Rodney pointed me to my own reality. No one can make that recognition for us, but pointers can help catalyze the recognition that occurs uniquely to each individual. It's a living recognition that continues to be fresh yet unchanging, regardless of the changing contents that appear.

There are two requirements for any outstanding book: a talent for writing and an understanding that is worth communicating. Rodney amply fulfills these two requirements in *Fully Present*.

His words emerge from the vast field of aware presence that is our true nature; they resound with the power of direct recognition and carry a kind of charge that can electrify attention to pay heed to the presence that is here in this very instant. *Fully Present* is a diary of daily experiences interspersed with reflections on nonduality. Unlike some books on truth which can seem abstract or dry, this is a richly sensual book with many flavors of experience painted in flowing, vibrant prose. Rodney demonstrates that recognizing the truth of one's being as formless awareness in no way diminishes the experience of form--quite the contrary-- experiences are even more vivid and deeply felt.

In *Fully Present*, Rodney debunks many myths; for example, the notions that self-realization means achieving an ideal personality or banishing unwanted emotions. Reading *Fully Present,* as well as *A Vastness All Around*, and Rodney's blog and interviews, has also helped free me of a fear I've had of being identified with thoughts and feelings. Identification happens, and it is part of life, and identification in no way diminishes the living field of presence in which identification and dis-identification both occur. When it comes to being what we truly are, there is nothing that needs to be fought or feared or fixed. We are 'water' and need not fret over any of the many wave forms that appear.

It is my sense that the only real sanity lies in knowing the truth of what we are. *Fully Present*, and Rodney's other writings, will bring more sanity into the world. There is a staggering richness of variety in all the particulars of each human existence, and I loved having an inside look into the particulars of Rodney's day to day life. Beneath the individual particularities of each human life, there is also a profound connection between all of us. When we read Rodney's words, if we listen closely, we hear ourselves. We know directly the truth of who and what we are.

Colleen Loehr, M.D.
Psychiatrist
Jefferson City, Missouri
July 25, 2011

January 2010

Friday, January 1

And so, the diary begins. I have no idea what will be appearing here. Given that my blog focuses on nonduality, these words will likely center on personal matters *in relation* to nondual ones. To have a strictly personal journal would, I suspect, be utterly boring and of little benefit to anyone. Also, this body/mind/personality happens to be a somewhat private one. Further, the entries won't be daily: My job and the blog prevent me from writing with any great frequency or length on anything. I do know, however, that the diary will attempt to show how, with the advent of this understanding, my life continues to be quite ordinary--but in extraordinary ways. So with that in mind, let's see what, if anything, emerges here.

Saturday, January 2

My girlfriend, Ellen, invited me over for dinner last night. She's a fantastic cook. She had baked a loaf of cinnamon and buttermilk yeast bread earlier that day, and the bread's sweet aroma still inundated her little 1950s bungalow-style house when I arrived (I walked over after work; she lives about a half-mile away).

For dinner, she sliced up part of the yeast bread and soaked it thoroughly in a French toast egg mixture. Along with the toast, we had Morningstar veggie strips (they look and taste like bacon, but aren't), organic strawberries, and cups of hot Bentley's green and blueberry tea. On the toast, we used a dark amber maple syrup. It all was so thoroughly delicious. The Christmas tree was still up and beautiful. Its light, as well as a slew of perfectly-placed table lamps, was the muted radiance by which we ate. Her lovely trio of cats--Midtown, Zoey, and Teddy--rubbed, by turns, against each of our legs. Then they were out through the cat-door to do cat-like things, despite the 35° temperature.

Ellen drove me back to my apartment after dinner, given not only that I have to clock in at work at 6:30am, but that I get up at 4:00am to make coffee, answer email, do Web research, and work on my blog. I am used to getting up at such an early hour because I'm almost always in bed by 7:30am. Ever since this understanding occurred, I seem to feel the complete *weight* of sleep, as it approaches. I can barely drag myself to bed in time enough to doze solidly off. Previously, I would get insomnia a couple of times a month, for which I finally got a prescription for Ambien (after natural remedies and over-the-counter products proved unsuccessful). I still have to sleep eight hours, though. And I still dream, despite the myth that 'awakened' people don't. My dreams are much shorter, however, and more like flashes of events, rather than the textured and sequential mental re-playings that I had previously. Untrue, too, is the notion that the 'enlightened' are aware of themselves as they are sleeping. Awareness can only be aware of itself through consciousness. In deep sleep, when consciousness is negligible (at best), awareness prevails. It only appears to be absent because of the absence of consciousness. This body *needs* its rest. So even if you could be awake in sleep, it probably would not be a very healthy thing to do.

Sunday, January 3

It is 23° Fahrenheit this morning, with the high predicted to be 39°F. I love it. If I were financially independent, I would follow the seasons: Go to Vermont in winter and South Beach in summer. I'm just an odd bird, I suppose. But then, every body/mind is quite different, while all is nothing but awareness, of course.

I actually visited Vermont for nearly a week in January some years ago. I found myself *thriving*, rather than depressed, in the dreary, overcast, and snowy climate. It would have been even more of a pleasure if I had known someone there who could have driven me around to some of those classic New England towns. But from my hotel in downtown Burlington (the state's capital), I was only able to explore the city itself, which included the frigid lakefront of Lake Champlain and the University of Vermont area (which was empty because the students and teachers were on Christmas break). In fact, I met not a single soul during my stay, but I was entirely happy.

Well, it is 6:00am, and I'll soon be off to work. I'm OIC (Officer in Charge) on Sundays, which means that I'm responsible for mall security until the shift-change (from 7:00am until 3:00pm). I work in Dispatch, as well as patrolling the property, and I observe and report things that are both normal and unusual. The unusual things (a suspicious person, an unattended bag, an alarm, an opened door) require my checking them out. The local police or fire department is called if there is any direct or suspected threat to the mall and its occupants. Being OIC means that I get to take my lunch break whenever I want, which I enjoy. I do my job, and then I go home. I've twice turned down the Lieutenant's position, mainly because it would involve my working evenings (3:30pm to 11:00pm). And given my sleep patterns, I would be thoroughly unconscious for the latter part of the shift!

Tuesday, January 5

Ah, the first of my two days off. The weather is cold (high today around 38°F or 39°F), and I've received a lovely message from my email-friend Peter. Like most of us, Peter's early seeking was varied and intense. In the late 1970s, he joined a Buddhist monastery in Thailand for two years. Then he went to South India in the early 80s and stayed, for ten years, in the Sri Aurobindo Ashram in Pondicherry. After that, he lived for another dozen or so years in the nearby community of Auroville, a universal city in South India where, according to its website, "Men and women of all countries are able to live in peace and progressive harmony above all creeds, all politics and all nationalities." Though a nurse by profession (he helped to run a primary health center for the local people in Auroville), Peter ended up neglecting his own health in his compassionate attempt to help others.

Now, he is living in various parts of Switzerland, getting his own well-being back in order and reveling in life "without a single question" (this having come about after reading Nisargadatta's *I Am That* and making some earnest explorations into select contemporary nondual writings, including my blog, I'm happy to say). He had been living for two or three years in Grindelwald, helping to look after a sweet eighty-something year old lady, and then had to fly to Pondicherry to settle a few business matters. Later, it was back to Switzerland, but this time to the hills of Lausanne. He has friends there with a large and lovely country house that he is helping to restore. My heart goes out to my dear and distant friend, as he carefully brings both the house and his body back to health.

Ironically, Peter sends me a long quote from Jiddu Krishnamurti's *Notebooks*, which he just happens to be browsing through (he doesn't yet know about my year-long diary). Again, it points to our close connection, of sorts, given that one will email the other shortly after one of us has been wondering what the other is up to. Part of Krishnamurti's quote runs:

"Meditation without a set formula, without a cause and reason, without end and purpose, is an incredible phenomenon. It is not only a great explosion which purifies but also it is death that has no tomorrow. Its purity devastates, leaving no hidden corner where thought can lurk in its own dark shadows. Its purity is vulnerable; it is not a virtue brought into being through resistance. It is pure because it has no resistance, like love. There is no tomorrow in meditation, no argument with death. The death of yesterday and of tomorrow does not leave the petty present of time, and time is always petty, but a destruction that is the new."

Peter's astute response is, "No, no, no, Rodney. He got it all so wrong." And Krishnamurti did, I'm afraid. Even when there is "no set formula," sitting in meditation with the expressed aim to become something that you already are will not help you to understand your true self in the least. For there can be no meditation without a meditator. So the moment you do any practice or sadhana, you are off to the binary races once again.

I just don't see how one can come to know oneself through his dualistic teachings, with--amongst other things--his emphasis on the observation of thoughts, feelings and sensations, and the great need for a "radical mutation in the mind." Self-knowledge does not require such a change; thoughts come up just as they did before, only now you know that they are not your true self.

Krishnamurti was obviously an elegant and sensitive man. But his teaching is not nondual, despite his constant urging to forgo all systems and paths. Also, his own understanding appears not to be clear and solid, given that he wrote from the position of experiencing *periods* of clarity, rather than clarity itself. Again and again, one finds him writing about a "flash of otherness" or a sudden "feeling of sacredness." I could say much, much more about the errors in Krishnamurti's passage here. But to what avail? He was, it seems, a truly compassionate and well-meaning soul. It would have been a pleasure to meet and spend some time with him, I suspect.

Wednesday, January 6

I rode downtown (Columbia) with Ellen, who had some work to do at her office (though retired from her job as media coordinator at one of the state art agencies, she still has a few light duties, which she loves). I walked from her office to the adjacent University of South Carolina campus, which covers over three hundred and fifty urban acres.

Due to the holiday break, there were very few students about. The sidewalks and brick-ways were long, empty, and speckled with light and shadow from the afternoon sun. With warm gloves, my father's army jacket, and a thermal undershirt on, I explored the campus. Then I went over to the Cooper Library, which is the university's main one, and it was open. That was great because the temperature was around 36°F, and I was starting to get cold.

Though I had not been to the library in over three years, I took my normal elevator-route to the bottom level, which is five floors down. This is where the Religion/Philosophy sections are. But I found precious little on advaita or nonduality. So I went back to the main level and perused magazines and newspapers in one of their newly renovated study/sitting spaces near the reference and circulation desks. Also new was the Cooper's Corner coffee shop, which, alas, was closed. I finally sat at one of the long wooden study tables right next to the expansive windows. There were a few students at the other tables. Some were peering into their laptops, while others were reading thick books with demanding titles. A couple of graduate students were talking just a little too loudly, wanting those of us within ear-range to be impressed by their term-laden conversation. But brilliancy isn't book knowledge or the memorization of large amounts of raw material. Rather, it is being able to recognize patterns and relationships in things. That's why I feel that analogy tests are one of the best indicators of true brilliance. Still, John Briggs is quite right when he notes in his *Fire in the Crucible: The Alchemy of Creative Genius* that "very few geniuses have exhibited anything close to spiritual enlightenment, aside from their work."

I peer through the windows, with their beautiful sloping vistas of buildings, winter trees, sidewalks, and distant views of the athletic grounds. Some of the scenery is blocked by the large concrete walls of another structure currently being built. I'm happy that they are able to expand, but I regret the loss of the lovely expanse. But nothing is fretted over, here. It was simply a particular feeling that rose up, and then it was gone.

And so was I, as I sauntered back to the arts agency, via the Horseshoe, which is the historic heart of the campus. This modified quadrangle includes ten buildings from the early 19th century, massive live oaks, and an array of brick paths that lead to various areas of the extensive university. The slanted light and architectural contours from the setting sun were hushed and magical. Except for two women walking their super-happy puppy, I was alone. I always try to come down here at this time of the year. I was afraid I wouldn't get a chance to do so this winter, but it worked out beautifully, as things tend to do.

Friday, January 8

No snow today. Or at least it's not yet here, at 4:00am. There was a fifty per cent chance that we would have some sort of "wintry mix," though little or nothing would accumulate, according to the meteorologists. Ironic, but one of the emails I received this morning was from a lovely woman in the UK, who says she regularly reads my blog. She wrote, with considerable polish and warmth, about the snow and cold there, which they have been in "the grip of" for several days now. Everyone is enjoying it though, riding sledges, and walking about with their dogs or mates. She walks with her dog which, she jokes, says a lot about her relationship with her mate.

For what it's worth, here is my morning routine: Get up at 4:00am, put the coffee on, exercise or do yoga stretches, wash up, get a mug of coffee, and go to my desk (which is my living room table). Once there, I check three different email accounts (where I respond to questions and take care of business matters), do a bit of Web research, and finally work on that week's blog posting. At around 6:00am, I put on my security uniform and walk to work at the mall, which is about three hundred yards away. On my days off, the routine is the same, except I sleep a bit later; to around 5:00 or 5:30am, if I'm able. And instead of going to work, I take a break around mid-morning and walk to the nearby Barnes & Noble (in the same mall) for some relaxing reading and breakfast. I don't people-watch, except for the occasional attractive woman or interesting person. When I read, I read. And if I had a laptop, I would indeed be working, and not *not*-working and wanting to appear cool.

Saturday, January 9

One of the first things I do before heading to the kitchen at 4:00am to make coffee is turn on NPR's *Music Through the Night.* This Minnesota Public Radio presentation plays marvelous classical selections, most of them Baroque, which particularly resonates with me. And then there is host Gillian Anderson's sexy, husky voice, though I don't have a clue what she looks like (which really doesn't matter).

Just as I was turning on the radio this morning, Arcangelo Corelli's *Concerto Grosso No. 9* was playing. I adore this piece. It gives hints of the numinous with its depth, nuances, and melodious repetitions. I've heard several versions of this particular concerto, and most of them were played too stately, which negates the piece's richness and vibrancy. This morning, it was the stellar Trevor Pinnock conducting the English Concert, from the CD *Corelli: 12 Concerti Grossi Op 6.* Another fine rendition of *No. 9* is the I Solisti Italiani's Denon recording. Alas, it is out of print, though our public library just happens to have it. And I will most definitely be checking it out!

Sri Atmananda Krishna Menon says that Shakespeare appears to have been awakened, given the extraordinary beauty, range, and depth of his writing. And don't forget his productivity. For he appears to have written *Henry V, Julius Caesar, As You Like It,* and *Hamlet* all in the same year (1599). Extraordinary indeed! I would say that Bach and Corelli (from whom Bach learned and copied) give indications of having recognized their natural states, also. It's nothing that I can prove or even defend with any finality. It's just a feeling, an intuition. But in the end, it really doesn't matter. Only their music does, their magnificent and luminous music.

Sunday, January 10

Ellen invites me over for dinner after work. This is terrific because her food is always delicious, and it gives me the opportunity to post my blog on her MacBook Pro. This evening we have braised asparagus (using extra virgin olive oil), leek and tomato soup, sour cream cornbread, and cranberry sauce. The house is sated with the aromas of all of the above. What a pleasure to experience this, as I edit and publish this week's blog. Then I'm off to the kitchen to help her. For not only do I savor good and healthy food, I enjoy assisting in its production.

People often ask about my being a vegetarian. Well, I've been one since my mid-twenties. I came across this bright yellow little book (whose title I can't remember) at the Clemson University library. It spoke concisely and compassionately about the benefits of not eating meat and the horrors that slaughtered animals go through. The book also listed the names of many well-known vegetarians, including Jesus, Buddha, Plato, Aristotle, Socrates, Albert Schweitzer, and Albert Einstein. I ceased eating meat that very day. I stopped because I could not bear the thought of ingesting creatures that had died such appalling deaths. Also, it was clear to me that being a vegetarian was clearly a healthier way of eating, provided you take care to get all of your proper vitamins and minerals. For instance, I take a multivitamin tablet each day, use reduced-fat milk in cooking, and eat eggs from cage-free chickens. And I still love desserts!

Tuesday, January 12

I slept in this morning (to 6:32am), and it felt *so* good. It was an active week at work. Yesterday, after coming back to the apartment, I followed my normal routine: I showered, washed my whites (colors tomorrow), and walked over to Ellen's to make corrections to the blog, as well as to explore the Web, and pay my bills, all of which I can't do on my ancient iMac. Ellen plied me with a hot cup of Typhoo decaffeinated tea and a maple-flavored scone from a batch she had made just a few hours before. Her little house, as usual, smelled like an old-world bakery. The scone was utterly delicious, of course--and I'm not even a fan of scones!

I added a donation note to my blog. I definitely didn't want one of those giant PayPal buttons. Some teachers and bloggers have them, and that's perfectly fine. It just wouldn't fit in with this blog's look and presentation. My note is a simple one, telling readers how to contribute, if they so choose, to my PayPal account. We'll see what comes of it. If anyone does donate, it will be deeply appreciated. For the money will be used for everything from groceries and office supplies (my printer has needed to be repaired for over six months now) to an inexpensive book that I've long wanted, plus my ever-increasing dental bills. But if no one donates, that will be fine too.

I'm off this morning--after working on next week's blog--to Barnes & Noble, where I'll buy some Starbucks coffee in the cafe, and peruse magazines and books. Now that B & N has free Wi-Fi, just about everyone in the cafe has his or her laptop with them. It must be nice! I'm actually very happy for them.

Wednesday, January 13

It's 11:00am, and I am back from spending the night at Ellen's. We went to see *Up in the Air* yesterday. I rather enjoyed it, though Ellen found it bleak and was at a complete loss as to how I was not depressed by the "sterility" of the George Clooney character's life and locales. The cinematography was excellent, especially the colorful and richly-detailed shots from the air. Ditto the acting and writing. I certainly would have fast-forwarded through a trio of scenes, but that is probably true of any movie.

Due to several disagreements (perhaps stemming from my reaction to the film), sleeping was all we did. Feelings of anger or annoyance still come up in this body/mind, but they never linger for long. They are simply seen as arisings in presence. Nothing more, nothing less. Momentary self-identification occasionally occurs to those who are self-realized. But appearances, whether they be thoughts or emotions, no longer define them. They are that which *recognizes* the thoughts and feelings, not the appearances themselves. With that said, Ellen and I are having more disagreements than we normally do. We really would be better suited as friends, rather than as partners.

I woke at 6:30am, made coffee, and went directly to the MacBook Pro. Ellen woke at 9:30am and, apparently having decided to fast-forward past my cinematic naivety, declared she would be making us breakfast. I usually have a late breakfast when she drives me back to the apartment, but she insisted on preparing a meal there. Okay, absolutely! She sautéed sliced mushrooms and diced garlic in extra virgin olive oil. Then she added dill, grape tomatoes, and several leaves of organic spinach to the pan. Just as the aroma of those ingredients was enough to make me salivate, she added six of her organic, cage-free eggs and scrambled them slowly, while pouring in a half-cup of silk creamer as she did. I was in charge of microwaving the Veggie Strips, getting out the place settings, and making my Folger's Colombian coffee (she had hot tea, of course). We heated some of her succulent maple scones in the toaster-oven. The breakfast, of course, was out of this world. And after it was over, I did what I do best: I washed the dishes.

Friday, January 15

A word about the diary's title. It comes from Chapter 45 in Lao Tzu's *Tao Te Ching*, which reads, in part:

> True perfection seems imperfect,
> Yet it is perfectly itself.
> True fullness seems empty,
> Yet it is fully present.

These words beautifully point to the fact that it is not 'me' who is now unconditionally present, but awareness itself. The body and mind are merely appearances *in* that awareness, and therefore quite secondary (which is not to discount their marvels and uniqueness). Ultimately, of course, the body/mind too is nothing but presence.

Saturday, January 16

I've been re-reading *Krishnamurti's Notebook* for the past couple of days. I say re-reading because I first read it around ten years ago. When I saw that our public library had a copy of the book, I immediately requested it, given that I was writing this diary. Even more importantly, it would be interesting to see my responses to it in light of my present understanding.

The *Notebook* begins in June 1961, when Krishnamurti started keeping records of his thoughts, observations, perceptions, and experiences. He writes daily in his diary for only seven months, and he writes mostly about a mysterious and often painful "process" that occurred in his head and spine, involving cranial pressures, exhaustion, and bouts of ecstasy. I have no idea what all of that was about, and neither, apparently, did Krishnamurti. He also records, in concise and lovely detail, about such locales as Ojai in California; Rome and Florence, Italy; and Bombay and Rishi Valley, India. About Gstaad, Switzerland, for instance, he opines, "It had been a beautiful morning, full of music and sunshine and shadows; the garden in the nearby hotel was full of colours, all colours and they were so bright and the grass so green that they hurt the eye and the heart. And the mountains beyond were glistening with a freshness and a sharpness, washed by the morning dew."

Ken Wilber's *One Taste* is perhaps my favorite spiritual diary, though I disagree with some of what is there (using meditation to attain self-realization, the weight he gives to states and heightened moments of awareness, etc). Still, it has depth, energy, and loads of perceptive assessments of perennial philosophy, i.e., the so-called wisdom traditions from the East and West. Fine, too, is the detailing of his relationship with his bright new love, Marci.

Sunday, January 17

Today's temperature got up to 61°. And it felt even warmer. The buds on the Callery Pears at the mall in which I work are no longer tight and grey, but slack and hairy. Ellen has already made two trips to Lowe's for multiple flats of yellow and purple pansies, along with bags of mushroom fertilizer. The cats loved her being out in the yard with them. They romped, sniffed the fertilizer, kneaded the newly-turned soil (still wet from yesterday's deluge), and lethally pounced upon anything creepy and crawly.

Tuesday, January 19

My day off, and I miraculously managed to sleep until 6:30am, which is normally when I would be clocking in at work. I got up, shaved, made coffee, and went right to work on next week's blog (having posted this week's on Monday night, at Ellen's). The blog was a combination of pointers and a review of Boris Jansch's excellent DVD, *Who is Driving the Dreambus?* It details the filmmaker's spiritual inquiry into nonduality by interviewing eight present-day teachers: Gangaji, Guy Smith, Tony Parsons, Genpo Roshi, Timothy Freke, Toni Packer, Amit Goswami, and Jeff Foster. It was interesting to see these teachers, many of whom I had not heard speak before because I am unable to access their websites and YouTube videos on my ancient iMac.

Ellen and I had a strong disagreement last week when I spent two hours on her laptop listening to various nondual speakers talk on their respective sites and on satsang.net. Perhaps she felt neglected. She kept asking why I was so interested in hearing some of the teachers when I already fully understood what they were pointing to. When I explained about my not being able to hear them previously and of my simply being a little curious, it still was not enough for her to see what I was saying. The evening ended with silence and tension. The next morning, I left. She called later that evening to apologize.

Some people for whom this understanding occurs can't read a single nonduality book again. Others continue to read spiritual books with abandon. I now can read only a handful of contemporary writers. I don't quite know why that is the case, but it is.

Wednesday, January 20

I tag along with Ellen as she makes her weekly excursion to Earthfare, the popular natural foods store. It's filled with people shopping, having lunch in the cafe, and working on their laptops. The bulletin board abounds with spiritual / meditative / life-coaching / massage / "cranial de-stressing" advertisements. There is also a group of a half-dozen people sitting around one of the large, metal tables talking quietly about ways to "deepen" their meditation. I try to do a little innocent eavesdropping, as I stand next to a green tea display. But some of the members of the group eye me suspiciously, so I amble quickly away.

This works out because I always go to the oils and lotions aisle whenever I'm here. All of these items are very expensive. Fortunately, they have ample tester bottles that you can try. Last time I was here, I chanced on the decadent *African Black Soap Body Wash*. This time, I discover *Goat's Milk & Chai Body Lotion*, which is so rich and creamy on my parched winter hands. It smells terrific, too. Indeed, I have to quell the urge to share the wonderful aroma with passers-by. I don't think they will take very kindly to my offering them the back of my hand, no matter how great it smells!

Friday, January 22

Yesterday was chilly and drizzly. The high was in the lower 50°s, but it felt colder because of the wind and rain. I loved it. Work, though, was busy, with lots of shoppers to monitor, given that people wanted to come in from the cold. I had to walk even more than I normally do. So I'm tired this morning, even though I went to bed at 7:30pm promptly. I'm going to try to go at 7:00pm tonight. But there is always the urge to get more reading done: Last night, I perused the *New York Times*, which I love because of the fine writers and the multitude of sections (Travel, Arts, Books, Science), and I tried to read Rick Bass's *Four Seasons at Home in Montana.* Alas, this monthly diary of thoughts and occurrences at and surrounding his home in Montana's Yaak Valley is replete with talk of his killing deer and birds, and his enjoyment of fishing. Bass is a fine writer. But this book isn't for me.

Saturday, January 23

I wasn't able to receive email yesterday morning. The receive function on my Outlook page just stopped working properly. I called EarthLink Tech after work. I got a guy from India (who was probably *in* India, as many call centers are these days). We had *such* a difficult time understanding one another. At one time, I had to go into my Security Officer mode: "Hey, stop shouting into the phone, please." He paused, apologized, and tried various things for almost twenty five minutes. Nothing worked. Finally, he said he would call me back in twenty minutes or so. He never did. Jeeze.

After work, I Googled the problem and found a couple of possible solutions. When I went to click on one site, my computer froze. So I put a straightened paperclip in the side port to unfreeze it. When I got the message about my "computer not being shut down properly, do I want it repaired," I clicked "yes," as I usually do. It did its routine repair. Then the thought came up, "Check your email," and I did. It was working again! Spam, queries from seekers, and an email from the library letting me know that I had books and DVDs awaiting me all came flooding in!

Sunday, January 24

I went to the Fresh Market yesterday with Ellen. While she purchased cinnamon scones and checked out cheeses, I sniffed the coffee beans in their big, sturdy barrels. The Kona Pure and Jamaica Blue Mountain smelled great but were very expensive. The best smelling and most mouth-watering to this body/mind was their Christmas Blend, which was still on sale. It contains vanilla, cinnamon, nutmeg, and spices. I probably wouldn't drink it every day, but I couldn't help but stand there over the barrel, sniffing the dark, glossy beans. I tried to get to the coffee pot, where they just happened to have some of the Kona Pure for tasting, but there were already four or five people waiting, so I briskly headed over to the bread section and started examining the sun-dried tomato and asiago focaccia. Ellen saw that I had already moved from the coffee line and, once again, my "impatience" annoyed her. Heck, it annoys me too! And she wondered, yet again, why this aspect of my personality has not changed. Because it's *my* personality! Personalities tend not to alter with self-knowledge. Indeed, I tell seekers that if they have some great insight and their personalities drastically change, then chances are it isn't the real deal.

Tuesday, January 26

My day off, and my incoming email on EarthLink wasn't working again. I spent all morning Googling the problem. No solution. I tried to chat with a person on EarthLink Support, but the chat function won't work on my primeval iMac software. Also, Ellen's cable connection to the Internet was down because the AT & T technician mistakenly cut the cable when he was burying her phone line *after* AT & T's contracted tree-cutters sliced her phone lines. Unbelievable! They may be able to get her cable connection back up this afternoon. I'll try to chat with EarthLink Support then, as well as post my blog, and pay my bills. Okay, that's it. I'm off to Barnes & Noble for breakfast and reading after a totally non-productive morning!

Wednesday, January 27

I was finally able to chat with someone from EarthLink, who was as gracious as he was fast and accurate. My incoming mail is now running smoothly once more. And if it acts up again, Mike D (the super tech person) sent me a copy of our chat for reference material. Utterly fantastic. I gave him a glowing report in the customer service survey that was emailed to me the moment our conversation was over.

Ellen's Road Runner cable connection is back up also, so I was able to post my blog last night. We celebrated both happenings by cooking and eating (of course). Actually, Ellen cooked while I continued to do a bunch of things I had to do online, which included research, paying bills, and adding Rupert Spira's link to my blog. Rupert is an excellent English ceramicist and nondual teacher who graciously added my name and blog to his link list.

Ellen made a delicious cashew nut roast with herb stuffing. A friend sent her the recipe, and it was a bit labor intensive, but Ellen managed it beautifully. She also roasted Brussels sprouts. This time she had me come over to see precisely how it's done: Everything from the slicing to the dousing with olive oil and garlic. The Brussels sprouts were so succulent that I started eating them directly off the hot pan as I took them from the oven. For dessert, I had a couple of squares of thick dark chocolate and warm, delicious green tea.

Thursday, January 28

It was sunny today, with a high of around 63°. I had a lovely email from my English friend, Fiona. I've included some of our email exchanges in my blog because she is an earnest seeker, incredibly articulate and, more often than not, comes to her own pristine insights with very little pointing or 'adjusting' from me. Readers, too, are moved by her words and beautiful prose. She sent me a digital picture of her and her dog walking in the snow. I was delighted to get it. For she knows how much I love definite *seasons*: Cold, snowy winter, verdant spring, hot summer, and crisp autumn.

In the email, she also told me about a Tony Parsons retreat she went to in mid-Wales a year or two ago. It was beautiful, she said, "all rolling hills, green fields, trees and sheep." Though she came to no true understanding, she had a grand time. And why not: There was, in addition to the three meetings a day, great food, great conversations, great walks, and lots of great laughter. It really sounds nice.

I actually wrote Parsons an email shortly before I started my blog, letting him know how much I enjoyed *The Open Secret*. (I also let him know that I came to my clear-seeing through John Wheeler.) Parsons didn't reply, not even a "thanks, now leave me alone." I explained to Fiona how this definitely rubbed my Southern personality the wrong way. Still, I wish him the best, and I couldn't be happier that Fiona had a fine time in Wales. For Parsons, it seems, really knows how to throw a fine nonduality retreat.

Fiona is presently having a fine time herself listening to some podcasts that John made, as well as (poor girl) going back to some of my earlier blog postings and perusing those. One of them particularly resonated with her: About how seeing or understanding come from the direction of presence, not from the supposed individual. She keeps coming back to that, allowing herself to be naturally paused by its pointing. "Happy" tears always come up, she says, and I think what lovely a thing that is.

Saturday, January 30

For dinner tonight, I had delicious leftovers from Ellen's cashew roast with herb stuffing and slaw (I make it practically every day using bagged, tri-color coleslaw and a coleslaw dressing). As I type these words, Ellen is driving over with dark chocolate brownies, with the firm dark frosting that I like. I am touched, moved, and *greatly* appreciative. Small and large gestures go a long way with me. It's part of my Southern upbringing, I suppose. We say "please" and "thank you" as easy as breathing. And when we say "thank you," we say it with a smile and from the very bottom of our hearts. And we certainly love good food in this region of the country. Fortunately, Ellen loves to cook also, though she's originally from Ohio.

Back to the brownies: She didn't bake the entire pan for me. She gave quite a few to her incredibly nice and very thorough furnace repair person, who was there today to do maintenance on the heater. And she also saved a couple of brownies for herself. But just a couple. She's still trying to keep the weight off, which is an on-going battle with her. I certainly encourage her to exercise, and am supportive in every way in that department. In fact, I never say, "Will you fix this or that tonight or this weekend?" That always comes from her, and her love of baking and sharing. And when you love engaging in something, there is a completeness in that particular endeavor. Or, as Buddha so beautifully put it, there is "no doer thereof."

February

Monday, February 1

The First Day of Spring. Every year, at this time, I always say that. Of course, it isn't the first day of spring at all. I just utter it to highlight the notion that winter, for me, is all but over. Today, though, is sunny and crisp, with the temperature in the upper 40°s. This silly and harmless annual declaration of mine is for me alone. There is little logic to it. If I were living in Vermont or Minneapolis, I certainly wouldn't be saying that at all, but there is a certain truth to the statement here in South Carolina.

Tuesday, February 2

After breakfast at Barnes & Noble (I sneak in a cinnamon muffin from the weekly batch that I make), I walk over to Ellen's to post my blog. A cold rain falls, and I glance at people through their warmly-lit windows, living their supposedly warmly-lit lives. Ellen is at the gym, and her three kitties are on various chairs and cushions within the house. It is completely quiet, except for the clatter of the gelid shower outside. When I go to my blog, I discover that the email that I sent to my blog from my home computer never arrived. My posting is supposed to arrive as a draft which, after signing in to my site, I edit and post. So I'll have to go back to the apartment (a quarter-mile walk) and see what the problem is. This means, of course, that the blog won't be up before 8:00pm. I try to have it up on Monday evenings between 4:00pm and 6:00pm. I don't have any hard and fast rule about this, but I'm pissed that the blog won't be up tonight for readers in the morning.

After doing a slew of Web research on various matters, I get hungry and go to the refrigerator, knowing that it is always stocked with scrumptious food. Opening it, I immediately spot (from Rosewood Market & Deli, the best natural foods store in the city) containers of curried tofu, broccoli and wild rice veggie medley, and roasted pine nut hummus. I have this with a hot cup of Stash Premium green tea. I take the tea over to one of the old, over-stuffed chairs and watch the rain continue to fall, as the day darkens. The tea is delicious and the hushness of the house radiates with presence. I take a deep, delicious sip of the amber elixir. Perhaps I live alone because of moments like this.

Wednesday, February 3

Busy day: Diarrhea, getting my taxes done, stopping by the library to pick up the books I requested (Rebecca Newberger's *36 Arguments for the Existence of God*, and Douglas Preston's sci-fi novel *Impact*), blog corrections, questions from readers, and a woman who wants to set up a time for a consultation when she next visits Columbia. She heard me on Urban Guru Cafe, and was surprised and delighted that I live here, given that she lives in Lexington, which is about forty minutes away. Later, it's back over to Ellen's for an early dinner (I'm working tomorrow) of home-baked scones and Ellen's incredible scrambled eggs. (That is, if my digestive system regains its normal functioning.)

Friday, February 5

Sprang my right big toe at work. Ellen, bless her, picked me up as I hobbled in the winter rain across one of the mall's parking lots. I didn't ask her to pick me up; she came looking for me after not being able to reach me on my cell phone, which stopped receiving calls after I forgot to get a new phone card. I went to Kroger with Ellen, who had to pick up a few things there, as did I. I'm back at the apartment now, having showered and taken two Ibuprofen. The muscles on the front side of my foot throb. From the perspective of awareness, it's almost interesting. This body isn't really focused upon much anymore. I attempt to take care of it, of course. I take my multivitamin/mineral tablet each day, lift weights, do push ups and some yoga. That is to keep it running as smoothly and as pain-free as possible. When it will go no further, that's fine. That's it. Consciousness dissipates from the body, and awareness returns to its objectless purity and is no longer aware of itself as presence (which can only occur when consciousness is present). Awareness will continue, as always. There will simply be the end of that particular wave in the water. The water doesn't disappear. Just that particular wave, that particular Rodney.

Tuesday, February 9

A feverish last few days of working, nursing my sprang toe, and getting this week's blog ready. The posting this week is, once again, an email chat between Fiona and me. It looks good, and perhaps readers will resonate with it. One never knows. I still have to correct a few omissions and make some grammatical changes, all of which I will do tonight at Ellen's on her MacBook Pro. Tomorrow is Ellen's birthday, but we are celebrating it today because we have more time.

This morning I made a batch of my world famous (okay, at least they *should* be) blueberry muffins for the work-week. I always give two of them (the box produces six large muffins) to Gordon, who is the ever-gracious maintenance and operations supervisor at the mall. My giving these days is done with a thoroughness and completeness that is quite new to me. Before my understanding, there would be the lingering notion of this 'someone' having done a generous and very nice thing. There was never an ulterior motive in my giving (he's a terrific guy, *and* he supplies me with delicious blueberries from his very own garden), but there remained this feeling that *I* was making quite a magnanimous gesture; there was this defined *person* doing the sharing. Now, there is just the action itself, without any labeling or thinking about it.

Friday, February 13

After work, I took my normal shower. When I came out of the bathroom (around 3:30pm) it was snowing! I put on my glasses and watched the snow fall, standing naked near the sliding glass doors (fortunately, drivers cannot see me up and behind the mid-level balcony). The snow was falling beautifully and heavily. I had no idea how long it would last. So I quickly made a cup of green tea, put my (still) sprang right foot up on the coffee table, and peered at the snow from my sofa. Ellen called, knowing that I would be thrilled. It was her three cats' first snowfall. I was especially interested in hearing how Midtown was reacting to it, given that he's Norwegian! It turned out that none of them was very keen on it.

I plugged away on next week's blog, while turning my head to the right every now and again to watch the snow, which increased in intensity. The stark and ancient stand of trees along the backs of the line of stores on the other side of the boulevard got dimmer and dimmer. I eventually gave up working on the pointers and opened the sliding door. The freezing air was momentarily shocking to the system, but I continued to stand there, with tea cup in hand, reveling in the sustained *whoosh* of the flakes as they fell heavier and faster.

Sunday, February 14

The snow was mostly gone by the afternoon. Today was sunny, with a high of 45°F. Oh, well.

Happy Birthday, Mom! I'll give her a call later this afternoon after work. She's in her 80s, and she delights in saying how she's still in full possession of "extraordinary mind power." And she is! It's always a joy to talk with her on the phone. My sister is staying with her now, and I'm happy about that. After Dad died over twenty years ago, Mom was quite content to live alone. Perhaps that is where I get my sense of solitude. When my sister's apartment complex in Silver Spring, Maryland, burned down, she had to move in with Mom. That was several years ago. So they are now helping one another out, despite their many disagreements.

I seem to function best living alone. Yet, I may end up living with someone. I don't know. I don't really give it much thought. The two things that I do a lot of (writing and reading) require solitude, at least for me. Even watching DVDs with someone doesn't appear to go well. I tried that with Ellen, and it was a disaster. We don't even like the same films; she likes romantic comedies and independent works, and I gravitate towards action/some horror/sci-fi/suspense and anything *Bourne*.

Wednesday, February 17

Spent the night at Ellen's last night. Before dinner, I checked on this week's blog and found a very nice comment from Suzanne Foxton. Her own blog is replete with direct pointing and fine insights, and I'm touched that she took the time to pen a response. I think of Suzanne as nonduality's resident "babe." It's about time we had one. She bellows with good-hearted laughter when I mention her lusciousness. For in addition to all of that, she is a loving wife, mother, and artist.

After doing a wee bit of blog editing and correcting, I had an exquisite dinner with Ellen. She made steamed broccoli and garlic, fake meat loaf, potato salad, and sweet potato flan, the recipe for which she found in a recent edition of *Martha Stewart's Living*. This morning, we went to the Original Pancake House for breakfast, as we normally do. It was great to have my veggie omelette, pancakes and coffee on such a cold day. And I had leftover omelette to bring back to the apartment tonight!

Sunday, February 21

Days in the 40°s and 50°s, and nights in the 30°s. I work and write. I received a nice email from Fiona, with whom I now happily and regularly correspond. She's ordering John Wheeler's classic *Awakening to the Natural State* and Randall Friend's *You Are No Thing*. Fine books both. But the answer is within *you*, not the books. And both books point to this fact. Yet, I can certainly testify to the glory of excellent nondual works. For it was a passage in John's *Awakening* that gave me a significant enough pause to recognize a presence that, for decades, I had taken no note of. So many people are seeking and struggling. I'm not trying to save them. I'm simply offering them--through my blog, talks, and books--opportunities to hear that their turmoil, confusion, and exhaustion are completely unnecessary. They can take that to heart or not give it a second thought. It really doesn't matter. But most of my blog readers seem to be giving it *considerable* thought and reflection. And I'm thrilled about that, for it testifies more to the quality of the readers, rather than to yours truly.

Thursday, February 25

Back from work. And I still have more work at home: Shower, make tonight's slaw, wash a load of clothes, answer more emails, and revise next week's blog. Is writing this diary becoming too much? Yes, yes, yes, and it's not even the end of February! Right at this moment, I want nothing better to do than stretch out on my sofa and rest until at least the clothes are dry. But there is no time. So I intensely labor. At least I've got some good pointers this week. You know that they are good when they are surprising and delightful even to yourself. What comes up nondual-wise, when I write or speak, is like a calm, steady emittance of words from pure spaciousness. It all just happens. Previously, there was a bit of effort to the writing, an effort that I didn't mind or really give much thought. Now, I see how much easier--*so* much easier!--pure creativity can be. There is no *me* doing anything. It sounds a bit fancy and esoteric, but that's the bare reality of it.

March

Tuesday, March 2

I spent last night at Ellen's. She's in Ohio, visiting family and checking into the possibility of moving there (she's found a house that she adores, and she would be closer to her family, since she was born in the state). She wants me to move with her. I'm happy that she does, but I can't possibly do that. My job and apartment are here, though I would certainly love the cold and snow up that way. But the state of our relationship probably doesn't warrant our moving *together*.

And yet, we are great friends and do terrific things for one another. I am house- and kitty-sitting for her, for example, and she made sure that the refrigerator is well-stocked with goodies. She left two kinds of my favorite vegetable quiches from Rosewood Market. I had the broccoli quiche last night, with organic spinach salad and yogurt ranch dressing. I sprinkled the salad with tamari roasted pumpkin seeds (also from Rosewood). I love those roasted seeds. I literally have to stop myself from downing the entire container!

I spent the morning at Barnes & Noble, after walking back over here to my apartment. It was great to not be working (security-wise) today and to alternatively read and watch the rain through B & N's giant front windows. For some reason, people are always curious about what I'm reading. My mix of magazines throws folks off, no doubt. Today, spread out before me, there was *London Review of Books, New York Review of Books, People, Blue Ridge Country, Poetry, New Scientist, Spirituality & Health,* and *2010 Travel Guide to Canada.* (I have cherished memories of visiting Montreal in January over a decade ago. The cold and snow were made even more exquisite by the beautiful woman with whom I spent those three magical days. We broke up, painfully, not long after our rendezvous in that fabled city. She is now married to a diplomat and travels the world in joy and splendor. I no doubt loved her very, very much. But I digress...)

Wednesday, March 3

Another night at Ellen's. And it snowed! I turned off all the inside lights and turned on the outdoor ones. The flakes were big and beautiful. Teddy (her large black cat) was silhouetted against the side window, as he slept on top of the over-stuffed sitting chair. Neither he, Midtown, nor Zoey (the sweet gray female cat) took the slightest interest in the white stuff, which started at around 9:30pm. When I went to bed, I watched the room gradually brighten, as the snowfall surged downward, turning the yard, woods, and sky into one of those folkloric white nights.

Ellen's bed was soft, warm, comfortable. It was a little strange being in it without her. But I wasn't lonely; I've always been somewhat of a loner. Yes, I will still (on rare occasions) miss someone, but it's more of a *witnessing* of those thoughts and sentiments, and not some defined state of bleakness. I remember reading that U. G. Krishnamurti once said that after he conversed with someone and they had left the house, they were completely out of his thinking. No further thoughts of them came up. Before my understanding occurred, I didn't see how U. G.'s words could be true. But now, I most certainly do. Speaking of U. G., he was a true spiritual genius, for he left his personal stamp on the issue of self-knowing. It's not that he necessarily said anything new or original about it, but his words were penetrating and uncompromising. And his perspective certainly was original! As is John Wheeler's and Sailor Bob Adamson's. One's slant, writing, and speaking about nonduality will be unlike anyone else's perspective, because every personality is different, though we all are nothing but the stuff of awareness.

The snow stopped at around 1:00am and didn't stick at all this morning. The day was cold, windy, and sunny.

Saturday, March 6

Ellen got back on Thursday. She had a great trip, though it ended up snowing here rather than there! Yesterday, we went to the library, where I had a ton of requested books waiting for me. One of them is Stephen Mitchell's translation of the *Tao Te Ching*. It's a slim, beautiful work. In the engaging and informative foreword, Mitchell speaks a little about the author (Lao-Tzu, about whom practically nothing is known, which is usually the case with writers and sages of genius); his translation method (he worked from Paul Cuarus's literal version, as well as meticulously examining dozens of English, German, and French translations); and the proper way to pronounce the book's title (*Dow Deh Jing*).

I've seen numerous editions of this marvelous book. And I always (especially after coming to this understanding) check to see how Chapter 25 is translated. In Mitchell's version, it is resplendent:

> There was something formless and perfect
> Before the universe was born.
> It is serene. Empty.
> Solitary. Unchanging.
> Infinite. Eternally present.
> It is the mother of the universe.
> For the lack of a better name,
> I call it the Tao.

This is pure radiance. The words are seething with grace and presence, and they give you pause, which is the greatest praise that can be bestowed upon any spiritual work. It is pointing to what you are at this very second. You can call it Awareness, God, Brahman, Self, or the Absolute. For Lao-Tzu, it happens to be "the Tao." What is it, right now, that is fully present, without beginning or end, and that has no name? You are the answer to your very own question. And that answer has always been directly before and within you. And it will always be directly before and within you. Simply see it for yourself.

Tuesday, March 9

I am continuing to enjoy Stephen Mitchell's version of the *Tao Te Ching*. I'll probably end up getting it for my personal library collection, which is small. I want to add to it, not because it would be a source of pride to point to when I have visitors to my apartment, but because I would like to have some grand titles in my bookcase. Both any visitors and I could then pull something off the shelf and actually enjoy reading it. It isn't easy to find nonduality books in bookstores or libraries. They have tons of spiritual titles, of course, but they are essentially self-help books. There is next to nothing on *ultimate* spirituality. But Mitchell's book is a fine one, and one that you can point to and savor. It also renders Lao-Tzu's words in a way that admirably shows what Sri Atmananda Krishna Menon once said about the Tao being perhaps the closest thing to nonduality and advaita. And you can easily see this when you read such elegant and *accurate* verses as:

> Without opening your door,
> You can open your heart to the world.
> Without looking out your window,
> You can see the essence of the Tao
>
> The more you know,
> The less you understand. (Chapter 47)

Or this concise and sumptuous rendering, as I've mentioned:

True fullness seems empty,
Yet it is fully present. (Chapter 45)

That last couplet resonates strongly here and is absolutely spot-on. The glory and "fullness" of the verse can only be seen, felt, and appreciated after you have come to an unmitigated clarity about who and what you are. As it stands, the verse doesn't make sense. Still, you are both moved and halted, even if you don't know why. And that pause is the bellwether of whether a work is one of spiritual brilliance.

On a related note, every all-purpose bookstore should have the following spiritual books on their shelves:

1) *Awakening to the Natural State,* John Wheeler

2) *What's Wrong with Right Now, Unless You Think About It?* "Sailor" Bob Adamson

3) *I Am That,* Nisargadatta Maharaj

4) *The Historical Buddha: The Times, Life and Teachings of the Founder of Buddhism,* H. W. Schumann

5) *The Mystique of Enlightenment,* U. G. Krishnamurti

6) *Mind is a Myth,* U. G. Krishnamurti

7) *The Biology of Enlightenment: Unpublished Conversations of U. G. Krishnamurti After He Came Into the Natural State,* Mukunda Rao

8) *Consciousness Speaks: Conversations with Ramesh S. Balsekar,* edited by Wayne Liquorman

9) *The Zen Teaching of Huang Po on the Transmission of the Mind,* translated by John Blofeld

10) *A Vastness All Around: Awakening to Your Natural State.* (Do you seriously think that I would go to all the trouble to write a book and not feel that it could be recommended to people?)

Wednesday, March 10

Got a nice email from John (Wheeler), letting me know that his Web address has changed because he was having some problems with the last one. I had figured that that was the case when I clicked on his site a couple of times this past week, and it wouldn't load. It is always great to hear from John. When one of us contacts the other about something, there is usually a flurry of long emails between us after that initial set, as we catch up and hear (first hand) what the other is doing. Then there is a long spell of not hearing from one another again. But really, that's okay too.

Thursday, March 11

Ah, the bright purple trumpets on the jacaranda trees fluoresce in the woods bordering the shopping strip directly across the highway from my apartment. They are semi-deciduous, native to Brazil and Bolivia, grow from twenty to forty feet tall, and tend to mix well with evergreens and other broadleaf trees. And that is exactly what they have done in the long stretch of woods across the way. The jacarandas flourish in the summer heat, but they begin to bloom in spring. I adore the fact that they produce such winsome florets even though they grow best in loamy muck. There's even a polluted, slow-flowing stream running straight through the trees' area. So they are, no doubt, making full use of the stream's availability. Each jacaranda blossom possesses a five-lobed, luminescent corolla that is damp and delicate to the touch, and hangs, choral-like, from the branches. The jacarandas let you know if they are happy where they are growing, and these are jubilant indeed.

Friday, March 12

Jeff Foster and I finally connected and put up link exchanges on each other's site. He is a really nice guy and has a terrific website, with tons of great pointers, color pictures, information on up-coming talks, and video interviews. He liked my blog, as well, and I was happy to hear that.

Saturday, March 13

I got a great email from my friend Peter. I was wondering how he was and where he was. Whenever I begin to think about him, I always get an email from him within a few days. I don't know how that is, but that's the way it happens. He's been back in Switzerland for ten days, where he said it is still very cold and with no hints of spring. He knew I would love hearing that! Before Switzerland, he was in India for a short while, and then went down to Melbourne, Australia for two weeks to see Sailor Bob. It was Peter's first living contact with anyone whose understanding is clear and vivid. He truly enjoyed Bob's "simplicity and ordinariness, no guru trip, no superiority, just friends sitting together and talking it over." He loved Melbourne too, which he said is beautiful, "very open, and friendly." The pictures I've seen of the place certainly echo Peter's words. I'm thoroughly happy that he got to spend time with Bob, with his down-to-earthiness and the directness of his pointing. That would be a joy for anyone.

Wednesday, March 14

I had a long and delightful chat with Fiona. She has Skype, so we were able to talk at length on a multitude of nondual and personal matters. She is vitally interested in self-knowledge, and she speaks and writes about her exploration with elegance and acuity.

The rest of the day was spent at the public library with Ellen. While she searched for kitchen design books, I got a couple of DVDs: *The Weather Man* (with Nicholas Cage and Michael Caine) and Jet Li's *Fist of Legend*. By the time I'd got back to the apartment and had dinner (frozen waffles and leftover veggie omelette from the Pancake House), it was time to go to bed, since I was getting up at 4:00am the next morning, and then heading out to work.

Sunday, March 21

Haven't written in a while. Been busy working and trying to bounce back from the flu, which isn't full-blown. Still, there is coughing, constant congestion, and semi-tiredness. Spaciousness is completely unaffected, of course. The symptoms, however uncomfortable, are occurring in a vastness that cannot be touched.

Monday, March 22

Ellen bought the house in Ohio and will probably be moving in October or November.

Tuesday, March 23

Didn't sleep too well. Once the body wakes and the brain starts on some train of nondual thoughts, it can be hard to doze again. But once I did, I slept until 7:00am. I would have stayed in bed longer, but I had to get up, make coffee, and work on the coming week's blog before a call with Fiona, which was at 8:00am. Again, it was such a delight to talk with her.

Wednesday, March 24

I came across a nice quote about Johann Sebastian Bach, saying that the key to his amazing creativity was just "ceaseless work...analysis, reflection, writing much, endless self-correction, that is my secret." That's all that's going on here, as well. The work, the reflection, and the editing simply get done. I write every single day, and it's the most natural thing in the world for me. Yet, I can't pinpoint a specific time or occasion when I decided I wanted to be a writer. I was just always surrounded by books growing up, and I always had a natural pull towards them, as well as to bookstores and libraries. On the other hand, I don't go into withdrawal if I'm not able to spend any time at my iMac (except to deplore the fact that stuff isn't getting done). The only time that I don't write is in the afternoons and evenings, when I'm tired and would much rather read or look at a DVD. And the DVDs tend to be action, horror, and sci-fi stuff. Really, I'm such a cultural light-weight.

Tuesday, March 30

The Callery Pears surrounding the mall are blooming with ivory and purple brilliance, and famished flocks of robins and cedar waxwings are inundating the holly trees and gorging themselves on the red, succulent berries. Sure harbingers of spring, both.

April

Sunday, April 4

Easter. I worked a solo shift. Ellen flew to Ohio today to spend time with family and even more time at her newly-purchased house. At the mall here, the Callery Pears' white blossoms have now turned a gorgeous lime, making the still purplish leaves that much more beautiful.

Monday, April 5

Rene Descartes' dictum, "I think, therefore I am," is occasionally disparaged in nonduality circles. It needn't be, for it isn't necessarily pointing to the superiority of either thought or the human sphere. I may be completely wrong about this, for I have only read a few threads of philosophical commentary about the statement. But Descartes' affirmation could just as well be pointing to Existence itself, inferring "I think, therefore I must exist." I *certainly* know that the statement would point to Existence proper if you were to simply turn it around and say, "I am, therefore I think." An even more accurate way of restating it is "I am, therefore thoughts arise."

It's also interesting to note that Descartes, whose interests ranged from geometry and theology to anatomy and philosophy, became less interested in solving *a* particular problem during his lifetime and increasingly more intrigued with discovering a "universal principle" that was the basis of all concepts and issues. Could he possibly have been headed along the nondual route? Very curious.

Wednesday, April 14

The daily billows of tawny pollen from the pine trees have finally subsided. Had a nice chat with Fiona this morning, as well as a funny email from Suzanne Foxton: My two favorite English women. Suzanne is one of the few nonduality writers with whom I correspond semi-regularly. Our emails are short, witty, and raucous. She'll read something on my blog that she particularly likes, and then let me know. And I'll do the same on her website. I think she would make a fine friend, given that both of our writings are expansive, that she has a great sense of humor, and that she apparently has a strong work-ethic. Now, if only she could manage to move hubby and family here to South Carolina.

Meanwhile, Ellen continues to make preparations to move *away* from the state. We are being extremely respectful and helpful to one another, including my assisting her sort through over a dozen dusty cans of fifteen-year-old house paints. I opened all of them, and those that hadn't dried, I filled with kitty litter, so that the paint would solidify over the coming weeks and be thrown (safely) into the trash.

I really should start putting more time back into the diary, too. I still don't know if anything will come of this. And that's okay. It's just that the diary is another form of work and writing, and I'm already hard-pressed for any downtime. All I can say is that there is this strong inclination to do it. The thought of whether it will be of some great benefit to seekers hasn't even come up. But if it is, I will be both thrilled and surprised. Then again, perhaps this inclination comes out of a sense of my wanting to show that life goes on quite regularly even after this understanding has occurred.

Thursday, April 15

I got an invitation to be one of the featured speakers at the Self Inquiry Discussion Group's (Raleigh, North Carolina) second annual retreat. The group, its website says, "provides an opportunity to meet with others involved in the search for Truth and Self-realization. Our meetings consist of an informal and open discussion of paths, teachers, techniques, philosophical and spiritual systems, and possible ways and means for expediting the search. The discussions are not academic or theoretical, but rather focus on our own personal experiences as seekers. There is usually also a period of silent meditation at some point during the evening."

Hmm, interesting. I hadn't heard of them, but the retreat sounds like it could offer some possibilities for clear and direct talks about nonduality. So I'm going to agree to be one of their speakers, as long as we can work out the travel details. I have no background as a speaker, no gimmicks or techniques. Yet there is no hesitation when I begin to talk about nonduality. Ease and readiness come *not* because I am naturally some great orator, but because I'm speaking from a fullness that is eternal and beyond containment. It is that to which all the great scriptures have pointed. And when that *Thatness* is in your heart and being, speaking about it is one of the simplest of things.

Wednesday, April 28

The Self Inquiry Discussion Group changed their minds about inviting me, because they don't have the travel budget to fly me up there or to reimburse me on getting a rental car. It's no problem at all, and I wish them the best. Because I live practically from pay check to pay check, I can't afford not to have my expenses covered. So the travel costs are the issue, not whether or not I get some huge honorarium.

Spent the night over at Ellen's, where she continues to prepare for her move to Ohio in September or October of this year. I posted my blog, while she made her delicious scrambled eggs (sautéed spinach and mushrooms in extra virgin olive oil, with fresh basil and oregano, parmesan cheese and silk milk added). I had some fluffy wheat biscuits with mine, and we had our tasty veggie strips, of course.

May

Saturday, May 8

Gaudapada, who lived between the fifth and eighth centuries A.D. and is known as the 'founder' of advaita/nonduality (he taught Govinda, who was the Shankara's guru), said that there are three "means to knowledge:" Reasoning, reading the scriptures, and direct experience.

Reasoning and a proper perusing of nondual books and scriptural texts can certainly *lead* to direct experience. But it isn't a step-by-step process; a + b does not necessarily lead to c. The direct recognition of your natural state occurs only when the reasoning and reading are naturally halted, and you see what is clearly before and within you. Thus, you can't ultimately stay with the texts or the reasoning and become self-realized. You have to take full note of that to which the words and inferences are pointing.

And a word about those Vedantic scriptures: I love how they are classified under *Sruti* (which is Sanskrit for hearing or, even lovelier, revelation), and *Smriti*, which means recollection. With *Sruti*, it is said that these ancient and anonymous sages actually *heard* the primordial sound of Existence (OM) and taught the *Sruti* from that. These teachings were eventually collected to form the *Smriti*. My theory is that the great sages recognized awareness first, and then taught that OM is one of the subtlest manifestations of awareness. But through the centuries, the OM declaration got badly translated in the *Smriti*. Then teachers began to tell seekers to meditate or to chant OM in order to 'achieve' this revelation of their actual Self.

Monday, May 10

Ellen and I had a delicious dinner: Homemade vegetable soup, biscuits, and spinach salad (made with a tasty ranch dressing), sunflower seeds, dried cranberries, and iced tea. She continues her plans to move, even going up to Ohio (once again) next Sunday to work on her new house, as well as to meet with contractors.

Meanwhile, my friendship with Fiona continues to flourish. It's such a joy to write and talk with her. Ellen and I are just wrong for one another (partner-wise), and we both have admitted to that, in varying degrees and on a number of occasions.

Tuesday, May 11

Morning at Ellen's. I'm enjoying orange sencha green tea, which has hints of Italian red oranges in it. This is the most delicious hot green tea that I've ever tasted. The individually wrapped tea sachets are large, beautifully sealed, and yet easy to open.

I've been exploring U. G. Krishnamurti videos all morning, something that I'm able to do only on

Ellen's MacBook Pro. Even on U. G.'s "parting message" videos, his clarity, humor, and sacrilege are in grand form. I guffawed on one section when someone began talking about the "sacredness" of the body. U. G. rolls his eyes in one of his "Oh, please" expressions and declares the body is interested in only two things: "Survival and fucking!" But he does point to the magnificent fact that there is absolutely no other body like his or yours on the planet. It is quite singular. Yet, it too, of course, is nothing but awareness. My body is what it is: Brown, tall, slim, and in its fifth decade of existence. I work to keep it healthy and in shape, but I'm not obsessive about it. With this understanding comes the knowledge that your immortality is already present, in and as awareness itself.

Thursday, May 13

As for Jiddu Krishnamurti (he and U. G. were no relation), I simply cannot understand what he's talking about. That keeps happening time and again when I try to read one of his books, which I sometimes attempt to do while at Barnes & Noble. After a few minutes, I get the clear but unfortunate impression that what I am perusing is utter nonsense. I don't mean to offend anyone, and I know that he has tons of followers. But if you closely read the talks, discussions, and Q & As, you can easily discern how utterly confusing they are. I don't know what he's teaching, but it is certainly not nonduality. Yet, his *Krishnamurti's Notebook* has some excellent landscape descriptions of Gstaad, Switzerland and Ojai, California, for instance. And many of the titles of his works are so winning and captivating that they almost compel you to open the book and see what's inside. Such titles include *Freedom from the Known, The First and Last Freedom,* and *The Awakening of Intelligence.* And finally, he seemed like a beautiful and compassionate soul. So I have nothing but respect for him and his legacy.

Monday, May 17

I'm over at Ellen's tonight and tomorrow, house and kitty-sitting while she is in Ohio. She flew up on Sunday, and I walked over here this afternoon after work, through pouring rain. My umbrella and the tall, leafy trees along the way helped to protect me from the deluge.

The house is quiet, and all the doors are opened. The rain continues to fall, though more softly now. The sound of it is particularly beautiful because of all the trees, plants, flowers, and fauna that surround and nearly cover her white, lovely, fourteen hundred square-feet home. Because it is small, the interior of the house is crowded, for Ellen throws away next to nothing. Yet, her place remains warm and homey, and I will no doubt miss coming over here.

Wednesday, May 19

I'm enjoying Ian McEwan's *Solar*, about a brilliant, Nobel Prize-winning physicist whose best work is behind him, and whose fifth marriage is in terrible shape because of his compulsive womanizing. Here is a particularly beautiful quote from a fellow scientist who is attempting to get Beard (the physicist) to consider taking a hard look at solar energy: "The [sun] drenches our planet, drives our climate and its life. A sweet rain of photons, and all we have to do is hold out our cups!" How lovely. And all that *we* have to do is simply recognize this *presence* of awareness, which not only drenches our everything, but *is* our everything. No real effort is required. Just see what is there!

Tuesday, May 25

Breakfast at the Original Pancake House with Ellen. There was some tenseness from a previous argument, but we managed to be civil. She talked a lot about her visit to Ohio, the "frightening logistics" of her forthcoming move, and how she enjoys so much about where she is moving to, in contrast to the throng of things that she dislikes here. I said hardly a word and just focused on my usual (and delectable) pecan waffle, scrambled eggs, grits, and coffee. After breakfast, we went to Publix for groceries, and then she dropped me off back at my apartment.

I'm now baking my cinnamon muffins for the week, while attempting to do some Web research for my next blog posting, which is getting increasingly difficult to do given the dated software on my iMac. On the other hand, the apartment smells *so* good from the baking muffins!

Thursday, May 27

Julian Noyce of Non-Duality Press graciously sent me a copy of Bob Adamson's new biography *Only That: The Life and Teaching of Sailor Bob Adamson*, which is compiled and edited by Kalyani Lawry. I've just started reading it, and it is a short, vivid, and captivating work. The first part is biographical, with the second section being extracts from his talks and teachings. Man, Bob really had a tough early life, with long bouts of drinking and depression. But he has also turned out to be one of the finest teachers of nonduality in the twentieth and twenty first centuries.

He tells a really funny story in the book. Every time I read it, I just laugh and laugh. It goes, "Watch what happens in nature. The lion will take off after a herd of antelope. Some of the antelope might have been lying down, but they get up and run off straight away. After the lion has caught one antelope, the rest will then get on with living again and eating. If the lion chased us, we'd be looking over our shoulder for the rest of the day saying, 'Shit, where is he now?'"

Monday, May 31

Lots of tenseness and disagreements with Ellen today. After leaving her house (I helped her with some gardening, and with disposing of a half-eaten lizard on the walkway, thanks to Midtown), I walked back here, relaxed, and watched the *Waking Life*, by Richard Linklater. Unfortunately, I didn't resonate with the movie. So I just ended up going to the apartment's Club House and channel-surfed on the thirty inch plasma television.

June

Wednesday, June 2

Bernardo Bertucci, who founded and runs the beautiful Laluna Spa, in Grenada, West Indies, likes my book and blog, and would like me to consider doing a program at the resort. I said I would (I'm solitary but not crazy!) and came up with a three-day program, which he liked and will offer to prospective guests to see what kind of response he gets. We'll see if anything comes of it. If it works out, great. If it doesn't, no problem.

Friday, June 4

Working hard on various things. Back at work. I was really tired yesterday, on my first day back (as I always am). Ellen let me know that she will be leaving for Ohio in August, rather than October. That changes things a bit, as I will need to step up my efforts to find rides to the library and the stores, and my getting a MacBook Pro. Yep, I'm decided that I will have to use most of my savings to get the Mac. I simply have to have one. I can't afford a cable connection at this time, but I can use the Wi-Fi at Barnes & Noble, as well as in the Club House. I'm thrilled about the notion of getting a MacBook, but not so thrilled about the huge expense, and so much sooner than I had planned! Oh, well.

Saturday, June 5

Bernardo emailed to see if I could possibly teach/host during *four* weeks in the spring of 2011! My nondual talks would be a part of other on-going spiritual-type events during those months. Alas, I won't be able to do the four week deal, because of my job. But wow, what a great offer! We'll see how many people sign up for the various spiritual events (not just mine) that Bernardo is planning. I have a feeling, though, that my talks won't be a go since I wouldn't be able to do the retreat for that long a time.

Sunday, June 6

Larry Coble, who lives in West Columbia (just across the river from Columbia itself), happened upon my blog, and has sent me an email. He would like to see if he can get some people together who are interested in nonduality and hold talks. I told him sure, if he can locate the people. I certainly wasn't able to do so a couple of years ago. I put up flyers, made announcements on Craigslist, and personally emailed some folks that I knew who had a spiritual bent. I got not a single response. Well, it worked out, because now I have neither the time nor the interest in doing weekly talks in the city. This body/mind is like that. Once something like that is over, it is *over!*

Tuesday, June 8

John LeKay of the new *Nonduality Magazine* (an online publication) wants to do an email interview with me. I started to turn the interview down, for I'm fairly swamped with the diary and the blog as it is. But John is a very pleasant guy, and the magazine looks good and has some fine-sounding people in the first issue, including Vicki Woodyard, James Swartz, Tarun Sardana, and the late Richard Rose. So I emailed him back--"Let's do it."

Saturday, June 12

Lots of stuff to attend to: The blog, questions from seekers, phone consultations, the ongoing email interview with *Nonduality Magazine*, my job...Jeeze, I can now see why Ken Wilber only wrote one diary (*One Taste*) for publication. It's work, man!

Monday, June 14

After work, I washed my whites at the apartment and then walked over to Ellen's through 98°F temperature (with a 100°F heat index) with my knapsack, another bag of dirty clothes, and a cloth tote in which to carry some extra stuff. I had a very busy week at work (the security truck was in the shop, so we had to do the garage patrols on foot), and I still have a final set of questions to answer from John, which I hope to do on Ellen's MacBook this evening. She has gone to Columbus once again to take care of some business, so I'm house and kitty-sitting tonight and tomorrow.

After getting the kitties fed and my blog posted, I feast on Chik'n Tenders, guacamole dip, and tempeh salad, washed down with cold black tea. Ellen got all of the above before she left so that I would have good stuff to eat. She also made the fresh jar of tea. For dessert, I had one of her vanilla cupcakes, with that firm, extraordinary, dark chocolate icing on them. She made sure that there were two in the freezer, so I'm having one tonight and the other tomorrow. Of course, it makes no difference what you eat, nonduality-wise. I just happen to be a vegetarian, one who hasn't had meat or fish for over twenty five years. I'm not bothered by other people eating a steak or piece of chicken in front of me, unless I actually look at the steak or the chicken, which I'm careful not to do. The thought of ingesting a slaughtered animal grieves me, even on a physical level. So I was thrilled to read in some recent report that less and less people are eating meat. With that said, you could be an avid meat-eater and discover this inner peace and spaciousness quite easily. And you may even continue to eat meat after your understanding occurs. Everyone is quite different on this.

Wednesday, June 16

Back at the apartment now. The walk back was hot, even at 9:30am! And now, it's 2:00pm and the temp is 100°F, with the heat index going up to 108°F later today. I'm still working on the interview and the final round of questions with John. Alas, I will have to be walking *back* over to Ellen's later today when the humidity will be at its worst (she won't be back until Thursday). But I need to make some corrections to the blog anyway, *and* I get to stay another night in her super-comfortable bed and eat her delicious good food.

Friday, June 18

The interview is up on *Nonduality Magazine*, and it looks good. John put it right up after his final edit. I thought he might save it for the next issue, but he moved some things around and put the interview up front and left-of-center of the home page. That was very considerate of him.

The afternoon: I'm back from work and, though tired, I bake some of my fantastic cinnamon muffins. They're cooking now and smell so good! I had to make them so I would have some for breakfast for the rest of the week at work. I still make the blueberry, but cinnamon has become my favorite. I'll make the blueberry ones for Gordon, the mall's operations manager and all-around nice guy. He loves them!

Saturday, June 19

Ellen called and wanted to know if I had any errands to run. I most certainly did. She drove me to the library, where I had to return a bunch of stuff, as well as pick up old copies of the *New York Times*, and Seasons 5 and 6 of the TV show *24* (I watch DVDs each evening while I'm having dinner). I also picked up two great Mac books: *Mac OS X Snow*

Leopard and *Teach Yourself Visually MacBook*. They are easy, interesting, and vibrantly instructive. Boning on this material now will allow me not only to work better on Ellen's machine, but to have a great working knowledge of my own MacBook Pro, whenever I'm able to get it.

We were having a nice time this evening. As she checked her email and did some other online tasks, I put together a delicious meal for us: All Natural Blue Corn Tortilla Chips, guacamole dip, tempeh salad, coleslaw, organic red grapes and iced tea. It was all nice and cozy, with the rain falling outside and cooling the hot and humid day down. Then we got into a major argument-disagreement about something. She ended up driving me back to the apartment, without saying a single word. Conflicts can continue to happen after this understanding occurs largely because personalities don't change. The only thing that *does* change is your total acceptance of a thought or emotion being you. They merely arise and depart. Little or nothing really lingers--and that applies to joy and happiness, as well. You don't even think of trying to get them to last because you now know that, by their very nature, there is nothing lasting about them.

Monday, June 21

I'm on jury service this week at the Richland County Courthouse, so I had to take the bus downtown today and back during torrid temperatures. And I might have to do so all week! This morning, as I waited in the already dense humidity for the 9:00am bus, I stood under the reinvigorating shade of a crape myrtle, with its verdant leaves and lush, rose-red flowers at twigs'-end. Petals adorned the ground, where they were falling onto the dark, damp pine straw that had been adeptly placed there days before by hushed Hispanic gardeners. Crape myrtles flourish not only in the full blaze of summer, but also in such harsh conditions as this torrid, fume-filled bus-stop and intersection. Indeed, the scene appeared almost Indic, with the brutish heat, the distant haze, the glorious colors amid the ground, and the trees with their fluted, almost desiccated-looking trunks. How apropos, given that crape myrtles are actually Asiatic.

Tuesday, June 22

Another long day at the Courthouse. To their credit, the powers-that-be go out of their way to make the jury process a tolerable one. Not only can we jurors bring food and laptops into the jury room, we can watch DVDs on a super-size TV screen. The movie shown this afternoon was *Cast Away*, that (mostly) excellent film written by William Broyles, and starring Tom Hanks and Helen Hunt. Hanks plays a FedEx employee who is stranded on an uninhabited island after a plane crash. I am always greatly moved by the end of the movie, in which he delivers an unopened FedEx package that he kept with him on the island the entire four years he was there. The house is vacant when he arrives, so he leaves the box at the front door, with a note saying that this package had saved his life.

He drives back through the bare, hot Texas landscape and eventually comes to a stop at a desolate-looking crossroads. A woman passing in a truck sees him, slowly brakes, and gets out.

Bettina Peterson: You look lost.

Chuck Noland: I do?

Bettina Peterson: Where're you headed?

Chuck Noland: Well, I was just about to figure that out.

Bettina Peterson: Well, that's 83 South. And this road will hook you up with I-40 East. If you turn right, that'll take you to Amarillo, Flagstaff, California. And if you head back that direction, you'll find a whole lot of nothing all the way to Canada.

Chuck Noland: I got it.

Bettina Peterson: All right, then. Good luck, cowboy.

Chuck Noland: Thank you.

As she drives off, Chuck notices that an illustration on her pick-up is similar to the one on the parcel. Chuck focuses on her in the departing truck. Because he doesn't move, you have no earthly idea what he is going to do. But you hope with *all your heart* that he follows her down that road--the woman who saved his life.

Thursday, June 24

I haven't been able to write much because of jury duty. Though I was in the jury pool, I was not chosen to be an actual juror. Yesterday, the court gave my group a couple of hours' leave, so I walked over to the main library on Assembly Street and got some DVDs: (*Glenn Gould: Hereafter*; *Rothko's Rooms: The Life and Works of an American Artist*; the horror movie *The Unborn*; and *High Tech Monorails*. I love these kinds of trains, and look forward to riding one someday, especially the TGV). I also checked out *The Long Discourses of the Buddha: A Translation of the Digha Nikaya,* which I ended up not resonating with at all.

Lots of great responses to the interview in *Nonduality Magazine*, including one from Colleen Loehr, a psychiatrist from Jefferson City, Missouri. She is a regular and astute reader of the blog, and we email fairly frequently. Fiona, too, was caught unawares by it, for I didn't tell her that I was doing it. I wanted it to be a surprise to all, and it was.

Tuesday, June 29

Emails continue to arrive in response to my interview (I added a link to it on last week's blog). I'm attempting to stay on top of the correspondence, as I write and edit this week's blog posting. And I'm so tired after work that I can barely manage to check my email, close the computer, and stretch out on the sofa, before getting up to make dinner and watch a DVD. Yesterday, I watched *City of Angels*, that (mostly) beautiful film with Nicholas Cage and Meg Ryan. It's beautiful until he "falls" to earth as an actual person. Then the picture starts not to work for me and I eject the DVD. I've seen the first three-quarters of the movie lots of times, and I now mainly look at certain sections of it: The library scenes, the beach scenes, the hill-top talk, and the dark hallway scene, where Seth, speaking for the first time to heart surgeon Dr. Maggie Rice, asks, "Are you in despair?"

Why is that statement so moving? Yes, Cage utters it with unblinking eyes (in case you didn't know, angels don't blink) and with heartfelt clarity. But more to the point, it is precisely the right question, because Maggie *is* in considerable despair over losing a patient on her operating table. And her response is just as telling; she confides (to a point) in this total stranger because she strangely feels an innate and immediate trust with him. It's a very powerful scene, and, like any work of inventive soundness, it holds up splendidly to repeated viewings, perhaps because it points to the despair that is in everyone who wholly identifies with his or her body or mind.

Wednesday, June 30

I spent the night over at Ellen's, having done my jury service for the day. I woke, showered, and made my hot organic orange sencha green tea, with natural cane turbinado sugar. Mmm, so very good. I worked on her MacBook Pro until she got up, when we went to breakfast at the Pancake House. After breakfast, I went back to the apartment and spoke with Fiona via Skype. Our conversations are wide-ranging, in-depth, and always interesting. She has become a close and welcomed friend in my life, a life that is largely bereft of such friends. I just don't seem to be good at making them. But again, there is no loneliness here. None whatsoever.

I finally took at break at around 2:30pm and went to Barnes & Noble, where I treated myself to a vanilla bean latte with soy milk. It was *so good*, particularly with all the mugginess we've been having (the heat index today was around 103°F). I came back to the air-conditioned apartment around 4:00pm, stretched out on the sofa, and cooled completely down after trudging along sizzling Beltline Boulevard. Later, Ellen invited me over for home-made vegetable lasagna, which was out of this world, of course.

July

Saturday, July 3

I've been in pain with my back for the past two days. I was getting up from bed and simultaneously sneezing (morning allergies). Because of the angle of my body, the strength of the sneeze, and the stiffness of my morning muscles, I got this sudden and throbbing twinge in my lower back. It is finally starting to get better today. But I'm continuing to take Ibuprofen, which (thank God) allows me to go to my job each morning, as long as I move slowly and carefully. And I *have* to work because every dollar is budgeted for bills, groceries, dental work, and rent.

    I had to struggle to walk up the hill to Kroger for more Ibuprofen, because Ellen and I haven't spoken in two days. She's still angry with me over some argument we had. She's got angrier because I didn't respond intensely enough. But really, nothing lingers here. She just doesn't get it. Our basic incompatibility continues to show itself.

Sunday, July 4

The back pain continues. I may have made the condition worse by going to Kroger. We'll see. Because it is the 4th, I am treating myself to new issues of the *Washingtonian Magazine* and *Shambhala Sun*. The latter is one of the few Buddhist publications that I tend to enjoy. Their articles are wide-ranging, the graphics colorful, the diversity of the people they profile and interview is wide, and they don't merely give lip-service to Dzogchen, which is often (and beautifully) translated as the Great Perfection. It, like advaita/nonduality, points to the natural and primordial state that is already within us. Unfortunately, many Tibetan Buddhists continue to feel that you must follow some sort of path to recognize this state. If awareness is already intrinsic, why the path? Indeed, any sort of practice *toward* it would only lead you *away* from it, because a practice can't negate the perceived person that is doing the practicing; the practitioner is just another thought. Your ultimate nature can only be known by the felt-recognition or understanding of who and what you actually are.

 I also bought the trade paperback version of Stieg Larsson's *The Girl with the Dragon Tattoo*. I've been reading so many good things about the late Swedish author that I decided to purchase his first book, and the crime thriller is indeed a page-turner. Larsson's other two works are *The Girl Who Played with Fire*, and *The Girl Who Kicked the Hornet's Nest*. I rarely buy books at full price, given the presence of Amazon, where I can get titles cheaper. But I wanted to get this book right away, and I'm glad I did.

Wednesday, July 7

Ellen and I are talking again. She called yesterday and I told her about my ailment. She came right over and took me to the grocery store so that I could get some things I needed. Then she insisted that I stay over there last night, because of her super-comfortable bed. She also bought me a hot patch, which isn't providing much relief, though I greatly appreciated her gesture. Neither is the Ibuprofen. So I've switched to extra-strength Acetaminophen, which I'm taking every three hours. And *that* is the only thing that is providing me with a modicum of comfort. Thank God I've been off for the past two days, otherwise I certainly wouldn't have been able to go into work tomorrow. The temperature was 100°F at Trenholm Square when Ellen and I went to the Publix there. And it's supposed to hit 100°F again tomorrow. I love it!

Friday, July 9

I'm enjoying Stieg Larsson's *The Girl with the Dragon Tattoo*. The characters (especially investigative journalist Mikael Blomkvist and computer hacker Lisbeth Sandler), the detailed writing (which goes on in places and could have been more tightly edited), the Mac computers, the fine pacing, and the intriguing setting (frozen Sweden, which is so different from steaming South Carolina), all make for a great read. The timing of my coming to these books (the so-called *Millennium Series*) is terrific, given that I can't sit at the desk for very long without grimacing. I can only ensconce myself comfortably on the sofa, or stretch out on it.

Yet, as I sit here and gaze out on the torrid afternoon, with all of this discomfort, I cannot help but reflect how wonderful awareness is. It has no form or appearance, yet it perceives, reflects, and expresses all forms. And it is as real to me as the throbbing in my back. The pain is there, the body is there, *and* presence is there. That is the only difference between my discomfort and that of others. Presence doesn't alleviate the pain, but it makes it more impersonal. You simply go ahead with living, taking as much care of the body as possible.

Saturday, July 10

It was an unpleasant day at work yesterday, with tension and an argument between another officer and me. I hate it when my temper flares. It just makes for an unpleasant situation. There are times, of course, when a strong response (personally or professionally) is warranted. But this wasn't one of them, despite the condition of my back making me generally irritable. Oh well, the deed is done. There is no denying my occasional petulance, which is an unfortunate part of my body/mind/personality. My temper doesn't flare up as readily as it once did, and there is no attempt on my part to control it. And a lot of times, it helps just to take a breath. The non-perceptive seeker would say, "But you're awakened! And you have anger issues!? How can that be!?" Well, I don't have anger issues; that would denote a chronic condition. My occasional vexation continues to occur precisely because I *have* recognized my natural state. If this were an experience and I was simply in some blissful mood, then I'd be smiling idiotically, and uttering the periodic "It's all good." Nonetheless, my splenic nature is there, and it's not a cherished part of me. Overall, though, I'm a nice and easy-going guy; even boring, some might say.

Friday, July 16

My back is almost returned to normal. I'm still taking two Acetaminophens in the morning. I am also gingerly doing some stretches and yoga asanas. Ellen made me brownies, which was such a magnanimous thing to do, and I was deeply appreciative. She gave half of them to George, her super-nice furnace repairman, who also does the yearly inspections of her heater. She told him that she would be leaving, but that she would be recommending him to the new owners. George is very religious, but he doesn't wear it on his sleeve. He is basically a happy person with a very strong work ethic (it even rivals mine). He apparently feels little impetus to convert people, which is largely an aggressive action from those who are insecure in their beliefs. And because beliefs and ideas are two of the least secure things that a person can have, such people tend to be tense, and feel easily threatened. George would be thrilled to pray with you, to talk with you about the Bible, or about his own conversion--but only if you brought the topic up and wanted to hear more. A true Southern gentleman, George.

The temperature today is around 97°F, with a heat index of 103°. It feels even higher. I haven't the seen the latest weather report, since it takes so long to download them on my outmoded iMac. I'm continuing to save up for my MacBook Pro. Some blog readers have made very generous donations lately, which may allow me to get the laptop before Ellen leaves. That would be--in the expression of the day--awesome.

Monday, July 19

The heat continues. The high each day has been in the mid-90s, with heat indices of 100° or more. I love it. Or rather, I love the fullness of each season of the year. When it's summer, I like heat; when it's fall, coolness; when it's spring, warmth and redolence; and when it is winter, cold and snow. How great it would be to go, say, to Vermont in January, and the North Carolina mountains in October. During spring and summer, I'd remain here in Columbia, with excursions to Charleston SC and Edisto, of course.

Tuesday, July 20

Everything at Ellen's is blossoming, as she readies her home for prospective buyers. The impatiens on the front porch are delicate and varicolored, while the acuba and cast iron plants around the side porch are bold and verdant. The southern lady ferns are flourishing also, thanks to the daily morning watering.

Ellen and I have tenderly broached the subject of us moving on to other people, now that her move to Columbus is imminent. We joke about it too, which is also good.

My back is gradually getting better, though bending over in the morning is still (quite literally) a major pain. Great to have the day off. I'm going to the Pancake House with Ellen later this morning, and then it's back to the apartment for a while, before I'm off to Barnes & Noble for a bit of relaxation and reading. *The Girl with the Dragon Tattoo* continues to go well, though the violence against women and animals is really hard to take. But there is no putting it down, that's for sure.

Wednesday, July 21

The new blog posting is up and Fiona, master proofer that she is, caught several errors. I hate it when such omissions occur. Sloppy writing muddles the pointing. The reader is left wondering what exactly I said. And the first reading of a pointer is usually the one that gives you the most pause. On the subsequent readings, your conceptualizing tends to be in full form. I am generalizing, of course, but that is usually the case. I wasn't able to make the corrections yesterday, though, because Ellen's car was in the shop, and it was just too hot to walk over. I may be able to stroll over sometime today before the evening heat hits. I really want the pointers to be as clear as possible and to pause the reader and seeker in an exceptional manner. That's the point of the pointers: To halt the reader's conceptualizing in such a way that he or she can see that not only is the pause suddenly there, but awareness is too--that one is just the other.

Friday, July 23

I went to the library with Ellen to both return and pick up stuff. One of the books I checked out was the massive *Foundation Grants for Individuals*. There might be something in it for which I can apply; my iMac could give out at any time, and my printer no longer works. Plus, I'm no longer able to open nearly sixty per cent of all websites on my iMac. So, I'm definitely going to take my time and go through the book during my afternoons after work. At Ellen's I helped her open more old paint buckets in the basement so that she could dry out and recycle them. The basement was hot and mosquitoes were coming in by the swarm, as I sat on the dusty floor, opening can after can. Ellen is a hoarder, and gets rid of nothing. Every personality is different. But I sure wish that she had dried and done away with all these paint cans!

Saturday, July 24

I received a nice email from a guy named Jason Sawicki who, it turns out, lives in nearby West Columbia and came across my blog. He is the founder of the Institute of Spiritual Awakening. In Jason's words:
 "The Institute was formed out of an overwhelming passion to serve all of humanity in

the realization of the true Self. Unlike traditional institutes, the ISA is not one of learning, but of deconstructing...of unbecoming. Spiritual seekers are presented with teachings from both classical and contemporary nondual teachers, along with the exploration of leading science in physics and cosmology, in a one to one or group satsang format. There is no price for any of the teachings, in line with the purpose of reaching as many people in the world as possible. The Institute will be continually looking for those whose realization leads them toward teaching, enabling the Institute to naturally branch out. In the future, the ISA will also be looking to sponsor many leading conferences and leveraging the power of the media in film to nurture the growing awakening that is unfolding."

Jason kindly asked if I would join him. I told him that I wasn't much of a joiner, but that ISA sounds commendable. I've offered to be available for occasional talks, if he wishes (for I am no longer interested in giving regular talks here in Columbia, as I was when this understanding first occurred). Jason agreed. In the meantime, he wants to meet for lunch sometime, which sounds terrific.

Sunday, July 25

I read another section of *The Girl with the Dragon Tattoo*. I'm thoroughly enjoying it, despite its heavy violence. I'm definitely going to start on *The Girl Who Played with Fire*. It's interesting that I happened upon an article in the *New York Times* about the 'Millennium' tours that are now being given in

Stockholm that take you to the actual places named in the book. My personality isn't one that yearns for that sort of thing. Yet, it might be interesting to visit the Mellqvist kaffebar (on the spacious, busy street of Hornsgatan), which was a favorite haunt of both Larsson and Larsson's fictional journalist, Mikael Blomqvist; and the hilly Stockholm District, which not only has fashionable stores and art galleries, but is the location of Blomqvist's small apartment in the brown, 19th century building at 1 Bellmansgatan.

Monday, July 26

After work today, I walked over to Ellen's to house- and kitty-sit, while she's in Columbus to check on her new place and the work that the contractors are doing there. I will be here tonight and Tuesday night. She came over yesterday and picked up some of my heavier stuff, so that I wouldn't have to take it over myself. She also, bless her, made a dozen of her delicious vanilla cupcakes with dark chocolate icing. She left some here for me, and she brought over close to a dozen yesterday so that I could put them in my freezer. My walk over here was slow and depleting, given the heat *and* humidity. Still, I will be able to use her MacBook Pro for two days, as well as eat healthy and delicious food. So it's a win/win situation for both Ellen and me.

Tuesday, July 27

I trooped over to Ellen's, pacing myself and taking the route via the air-conditioned mall and some shady spots along the streets. It's morning now and comfortable, though today's heat index is going to be its typical 100° plus. All the doors are opened and the fans are on in her cozy little house. It's great to be able to check this morning's blog and to tap out this diary entry on her MacBook, with its super-comfortable keyboard. I checked the blog, paid bills, and examined a couple of nondual sites and blogs.

And speaking of blog-stuff, it's interesting how pointers come to me: The best ones appear while I'm doing such ordinary stuff as shaving, showering, or washing my hands. It was doing the latter that this question came to me:

"How can there be a path to what you already are?"

Now *that's* a stellar pointer. It immediately curbs your conceptualizing, and the pause can be substantial enough for a full recognition of your ever-present Self. Some Zen/nondual teachers say that you need to be shocked into seeing, but that's not necessary at all. I mean, it can work, but it's not imperative. All that is needed is for one's thinking to be naturally paused and then cognizing what is *immediately* present within that pause.

Wednesday, July 28

It was nice spending another night at Ellen's. And it wasn't as hot as it has been when I walked back over today. I spent the morning working on next week's blog, making blueberry muffins for the week, and going to Barnes & Noble (where I can no longer eat my muffins because B & N corporate has recently come down on them about allowing people to bring food into the store). Dang.

Back at Ellen's, I sit on the porch as a blustery storm approaches, with much wind, lightning, and thunder. It is very relaxing to sit in this welcoming, screened-in area with its creaky swing and weathered wooden rockers. The porch is made even snugger by the fact that the house is surrounded by oaks, elms, and pines of widely varying ages. So, as I peer up from my chair, I can only see higher and abutting trees, cascading branches, flying leaves, and the innumerable tufts of things being carried by parched, zephyr-like squalls.

My spaciousness extends fully beyond the porch, the trees, and the sky, of course. And it is not so much extending from me as it is enfolding all that I can see or conceive of. Awareness is in the winds, and the winds are in awareness. All is presence.

When the downpour finally arrived, I opened up the doors, turned on the overhead fans, and read the final portion of *The Girl with the Dragon Tattoo*, as I listened to the drenching rain outside. It and Larsson's prose were very moving indeed. It was great to have a reprieve from the violence in that last portion of the book. I went to sleep later, as the rain continued to fall. The window was opened so all through the night I could hear the plummeting drops striking the green masses of leaves.

Thursday, July 29

Back from work and exhausted, as I always am after the first day. The exhaustion is compounded by the heat. I immediately started reading the second Larsson book in the 'Millennium' series, *The Girl Who Played with Fire*. This time I'm just going to skip the overly violent portions. Why would anyone want to raise those thoughts and images in one's head?

Friday, July 30

Creativity is that which cannot be contained. It is the doing of something that feels wholly natural and pleasing, with no ulterior motive. Then your work, art, or practice is filled with nuance, elegance, and finality. Such works approach--or even attain-- unequivocal brilliance. Writing, music, sculpture, photography, architecture, and sustainable living and design are just a few fields in which creativity plays a primary role. Other such areas include teaching, translation, and even history, all of which are often given short shrift. One of my favorite books is *The Historical Buddha: The Times, Life and Teachings of the Founder of Buddhism*, by H. W. Schumann. Here you have a volume that is largely bereft of myths and legends. Schumann attempted to capture a man who was, at once, enigmatic and ordinary. For instance, Buddha, through his sometimes rote life texts, appears as if he was some bland, easy-going guy. But we learn from specific historical accounts that he had a dynamic personality and lots of charisma. Also, he is often thought to be omniscient by his followers, but he himself uttered, "No one knows everything." So we can see here how history can be creative, accurate, and moving.

August

Monday, August 2

In Sanskrit, yoga translates as "to yoke." To me, that means to yoke or unite breath with movement, rather than body with universal spirit or higher self. Yes, yoga denotes lots of things to lots of people. But I think the above is closer to its true and classical meaning. It's certainly not aerobics! But if people want to practice it that way, power to them. I continue to do and enjoy yoga several times a week myself. And all stretches, holds, and twists are done in seamless coordination with the breath.

I got my Yoga Teacher's Training Certificate in August 1979, at Ananda Ashram, in Monroe, New York. The director and head instructor was Ramamurti S. Mishra, M.D., who was a neurosurgeon, yoga teacher, Sanskrit scholar, and author, known for his classics *Fundamentals of Yoga* and *The Textbook of Yoga Psychology*. Dr. Mishra later changed his name to Shri Brahmananda Sarasvati, which was more in line with the ashram itself which, as the website notes, was "founded on the universal principles of Yoga and Vedanta and dedicated to East-West cultural exchange. Our classes center around Hatha Yoga, Sanskrit, and Ayurveda." Dr. Mishra was a pleasantly demanding teacher, and a man of good cheer. With my teaching certificate, I was able to teach yoga for a while and earn a semi-decent living doing it.

Tuesday, August 3

Non-Duality Press now wants to publish my manuscript as an eBook, instead of a paperback. Their earlier comments about the manuscript were quite positive, suggesting that they were considering publishing it as a regular trade paperback. But now the eBook offer! I told them, "Forget it." For I want people to be able to hold the published tome in their hands. Well, that's probably it, as far as the book goes, for I have neither the time nor the inclination to send it out to a slew of other publishers and wait around for their decisions. Also, I'm going to have to decide how long I want to continue this diary which, of course, was going to be fodder for *another* title!

Thursday, August 5

I haven't been much in the mood to write over the past couple of days. I may not even post a blog this week, after having steadily produced one each week since 2008. We'll see how it goes. I certainly have no impulse to do it at the moment.

Friday, August 6

Ellen invited me over for dinner yesterday. I went into no details about Non-Duality Press not wanting to do *Vastness* as a paperback. There seemed to be no point, given her lack of interest in nonduality and my blog. Still, her cooking skills are marvelous. She made a thick and delicious soup from vegetables purchased at one of the local farmers' markets, and a delicious blueberry 'n' cheese coffee cake. And we had lots of her bracing iced tea, which was a good thing too: It was 99°F in the shade. The coffee cake was a moist blueberry cream cheese cake with a crusty, lemon-sugar topping. We laughed at how oddly well the cake went with the vegetables!

Saturday, August 7

I had a nice long chat with a Particular Nonduality Teacher yesterday. He called me using Skype, so he was practically able to talk for free. I told him about Non-Duality Press, and he immediately suggested that I self-publish the manuscript, which was a great idea. He further suggested that he would help me set up an account at Lulu and get me an online presence at Amazon. But all this is dependent upon my being able to change the manuscript file from PDF (which I should *not* have sent to Non-Duality Press, the teacher informed me, because they would not have been able to edit on it) to RTF (since Ellen doesn't have MS Word on her laptop). And after that, the manuscript would require, according to him, at least ninety hours of editing and formatting work to get it ready for Lulu. He doesn't think he has the energy to do that, and I certainly understand.

Tuesday, August 10

I emailed P. N. T. today, saying that I want to proceed with getting *Vastness* in shape and ready to be published via Lulu. Earlier, I had sent him an email declining to do it. Also, J. D. Hazelwood, whose fine books are published by Lulu, convinced me that it was okay to proceed. Basically, I'm going to spend this week writing and adding an acknowledgements page, as well as editing and adding the interview I did for *Nonduality Magazine*. And Fiona, bless her, asked if I would like her to proof it, and I *absolutely* would. I didn't want to ask her unless she raised the issue of wanting to do it, and she did just that in our call this morning!

There is *so* much work to do. But the upside is that it will be divided between me, Fiona, and P. N. T. It shouldn't take more than a week or two. Then again, I could seriously be underestimating things. We'll see.

Thursday, August 12

I had another extended phone conversation with P. N. T. about the book. He told me the manuscript needs to be turned into a Word file and completely reformatted if I want a 6x9 book, instead of an 8.5x11. Well, I definitely don't want a book with *those* dimensions. It would be odd looking and couldn't be carried and held comfortably.

Alas, I can't find a way to change the manuscript to 6x9 on Ellen's MacBook Pro. Even Googling the question provides no clear answer. And I've already spent a great deal of time trying to do all of this yesterday over at Ellen's, after we ran a bevy of errands in the 97°F heat, so I'm more drained than normal.

Saturday, August 14

Working hard, despite my having gotten what Ellen had, which is some kind of lingering chest or throat infection. I'm taking antihistamines every morning, as well as coughing and blowing my nose throughout the day.

Sunday, August 15

Fiona is doing a terrific job of proofing the manuscript. It's a herculean task, given that I make so many grammatical and omission errors. I catch as many as I can, but there always seem to be more that require ferreting out. I'm depleted from my job, the book, *and* the throat infection. All my body wants to do right now is rest. But I can't. There is entirely too much work to do!

Thursday, August 19

P. N. T. and I have exchanged some emails, as I continue to work on the book. He won't be able to do the 6x9 converting for me. He says that he just doesn't have the energy these days, and I certainly understand.

After some intense Googling, I came upon the name of Greg Banks, of BDDesign LLC: The Self Published Author's Best Friend. Greg, it turns out, is just that. For he not only offered to do the 6x9 converting for me, but he will also make sure that the book appears great after the converting is done. Greg is very knowledgeable about Lulu, and he explains very clearly how things should be done, which is very much needed here, since my computer skills are miniscule. And he is charging me as little as possible, since he knows that I have very little money.

Fiona wants to do a final edit of the book once I finish it. I told her that I had already gone over the acknowledgements page and the *Nonduality Magazine* interview. But she (wise woman) doesn't trust my having fresh eyes and wants to give it a final go-over. I'm thrilled that she wants to do it, and the book will greatly benefit by it.

Sunday, August 22

I've been walking over to Ellen's after each work day to toil on my manuscript. It continues to need a lot of corrections and honing. The walking is hard in itself, given the 100° heat indices. Also, it's a half-mile away, and a good half of that is uphill. I don't want to have Ellen pick me up, because she is very busy with preparing to put the house up for sale. After working all yesterday afternoon, Ellen and I went to Hooligan's, where I had an absolutely delicious veggie burger, fries, honey mustard on the side (weird, I know, but it's what I love), and a tall cup of Sprite. It all tasted *so* good, given the walk, heat, and intense writing and editing. Ellen and I then went by the library. She had books to return, and I had things to pick up: Used copies of the *New York Times*, and the DVDs *The Ghost Writer* and the TV series *Flashforward*.

Tuesday, August 24

This is the first cool morning of the season. I'm staying with Ellen, who is still sleeping. I have all the doors and windows open, and the house fan is on. It feels so nice, no heat and humidity for a change. I sip my warm and flavorful organic green tea as I type.

Wednesday, August 25

I have had a *huge* disagreement with P. N. T. regarding the book. There is no need to go into details. It's enough to say that that friendship is over. There are no deep regrets or deep anger coming up here. I wish him the best, but I have absolutely no desire to talk or write to him again.

 Meanwhile, I signed up at Lulu and immediately saw that it's going to take me more than a while to understand how the process works. I'm going to have to figure it all out myself. Meanwhile, Fiona has finished yet another proof of the manuscript and sent it to me. I, in turn, will be sending it to Greg Banks tomorrow so that he can convert it; he'll also make sure that the manuscript looks right after that. Greg has been a pleasure to work with, and I wish that I could afford to have him help me with more of the Lulu stuff. But he's already giving me a break on the pricing, and I'm so thankful for that, I don't want to ask any additional questions, for he's already answered more than a few.

Friday, August 27

Continuing to trudge over to Ellen's through the heat and humidity each day after work. Exhaustion is starting to set in again. I'm having to both labor steadily on the manuscript and familiarize myself with Lulu. On the way back to my apartment this afternoon, Ellen and I stop at Zesto's (a kind of fast-food dairy bar), which is midway between my apartment and her house. She treats us to chocolate-dipped vanilla ice cream cones. She gets chocolate and I vanilla. Well, it was supposed to have been vanilla, but the clerk misunderstood me, and I get a vanilla/chocolate swirl. I don't care. I am so hot and tired that ice cream tastes like manna from the gods. I hadn't been in here for a while. Sometimes I come here to get ice cream and, occasionally, their Grilled-Cheese Baskets: A grilled cheese sandwich, fries, and slaw. I'll get this with their iced tea. Then I like to watch, through the large plate-glass window, the heat, and the heavy traffic at the stop-light on Forest Drive. The mall where I work is almost directly across the street. So everything is quite near. Still, I only eat here in the summer, when I can sit in one of their cool booths and watch the people and traffic come and go through the torrid intersection.

Tuesday, August 31

I sent the final edit of the book to Greg Banks on the 27th. He's still working on it, thank goodness. For this gives me time to explore the Lulu site, see what needs to be done, and to have all my other information ready to go when Greg sends me the PDF to approve. It has also given me time to put questions up on the forum, and I'm so moved when I receive emailed answers to those questions over a series of days; generous, compassionate, and knowledgeable people taking the time to tell me how to do the simplest of things on Lulu. It's fantastic, and I wish I could hug every one of them.

Last night, it got down to around 60°F. It was nice and cool this morning (I stayed over at Ellen's). The leaves on the trees are starting to hint at their future turning, with tinges of brown and pale green. The days are still in the low to mid 90s, but without the draining humidity.

Ironically, I came across a great quote from Nietzsche's *Human, All Too Human* today: "All great artists and thinkers [are] great workers, indefatigable not only in inventing, but also in rejecting, sifting, transforming, ordering." Yes indeed. All of these things occur on their own. Someone looking on might think that all my actions are pure effort, but they are not. My body is often tired, even totally fatigued, but this writing remains the most natural of things. I spend hours and hours each day writing and re-writing at the computer. But the time-element really doesn't figure into it. It's like reading: I look up at the clock, and I'm *amazed* at what time has passed, however depleted my body may feel. This has particularly been the case since this understanding occurred.

September

Thursday, September 2

Ellen and I went to the always inviting Trenholm Square, where we shopped at Publix and the Fresh Market. From the latter, she purchased some expensive Kona Blend decaf and made French press coffee back at her place. The coffee was *so* good! And I told her as much. She joked that if she does happen to meet someone, he probably won't appreciate her food as much as I do. She is certainly right about that!

Friday, September 3

Ellen called me after her appointment with her acupuncturist. She said that she was looking at her Volkswagen's thermometer, and it was 100°F in the shade. God knows what the heat index is. She phoned to see if I wanted her to pick me up so that I could go over to the house to work on the MacBook. That was really very sweet of her, but I was too tired and told her that I would come over tomorrow. No doubt my body was trying to say, "Enough already!" It's like doing two jobs, back-to-back: My morning security job, and then my afternoon task of completing the book. Right now, I couldn't move, focus, or do a single line edit even if I wanted to.

On the positive side, Ellen and I have been getting along much better now that we know that she is definitely moving, and that we probably will be seeing other people. I've been helping her with bunches of things, house-wise, yard-wise, and kitty-wise. And she has tolerated my extended periods on her MacBook Pro when I'm over there. The hours just hurtle by when I am working on it. I never seem to have enough time to do everything. So I'm deeply appreciative of her understanding and generosity.

Sunday, September 5

Ah, a turning-of-the-days: The sun is bright, but the breezes are refreshing and the humidity is lower. And some of the leaves on the maples are already yellow. I still feel an intense connection with the seasons. There is something deep and pristine about this time of the year, and that connection is made even more mesmerizing with the autumnal display of colors and coolness. Presence, of course, is completely unaffected by this. All of existence is happening *within* it. And yet, every single leaf is a manifestation of awareness itself. How moving indeed.

Tuesday, September 7

I am at Ellen's, having walked over after a busy day at work. She had to make another trip to Columbus to check on work being done at her new home. So, once again, I'm house and kitty-sitting for the next two days--getting to work on the MacBook Pro, of course!

Ellen left a slew of little surprises for me. When I went to grab my bag of dirty clothes that I gave her to bring over here so that I could wash them, she had left a note on top of the bag saying, "These are now clean!" She had folded everything, too! And in the kitchen, she left the refrigerator packed with some of my favorite things from Publix and Rosewood Market. The goodies included Southern potato salad, tempeh salad, organic coleslaw, tamari roasted pumpkin seeds, organic red grapes (firm yet bursting with juice and flavor), guacamole veggie dip, Morning Star Chik'n Tenders for dipping into the guacamole dip, and nearly a dozen of her incredibly delicious frosted cupcakes in the freezer (one of which I have thawing as I type).

But there's more! She purchased a bar of the Tom's of Maine moisturizing soap that I love. And perhaps most important of all, knowing of my recent bouts of insomnia, she left a bottle of Swanson's Homeopathic Insomnia Relief on the kitchen counter. It is supposed to temporarily relieve sleeplessness. I will certainly give two tablets a try tonight, though I am plenty tired already from work and walking over in the heat.

I also found a bag of Pirate's Booty Veggie Baked Rice and Corn Puffs. They are all natural and trans fat free. Man, are they good! Again, I'm floored both by Ellen's thoughtfulness and generosity, as well as the comfort in her grand little house. I wish she weren't leaving, but the move is pretty much a done deal.

Thursday, September 9

Went for my annual eye exam and to renew my contacts prescription. Though I'm quite nearsighted, my prescription has remained the same and not gotten worse for a sixth or seventh year. I really enjoy going to Dr. Joi Tyler, the optometrist, who has an office in LensCrafter's at the mall. Though we know virtually nothing about one another, we have an easy camaraderie. Because she had to dilate my eyes, everything is intensely bright. She gave me some cool shades to wear back to the apartment. Even the light coming in from the balcony is too bright and uncomfortable; I close the blinds and re-watch *Sri Nisargadatta Maharaj: The Lost Satsang*. I don't watch it all, just most of it. I love the section where he exclaims, when a seeker begins to ask a follow-up question to a semi-related issue, "Just do what I say! All your questions are sprouting from your identification with the body-form." Precisely. You take yourself to be your thoughts, feelings, and physicality. Thus, all of these inane and troublesome questions pop up, questions that can't possibly be squared with what you read or hear about presence. Because of the mismatch, you give emphasis to the questions rather than to the teacher's pointing, which is directing you to an actuality *beyond* the question. As for legitimate queries: If you give your clear attention to the significance and immediacy of the teacher's words, your questions will be the 'right' ones; that is, lucid, heartfelt, and at the very edge of Knowingness.

Sunday, September 12

Greg finished the reformatting of the manuscript, and he did a stellar job. There were so many little (and large) things that he took care of that I simply would have forgotten or not known about. The only frustration is that I've been too tired to go over to Ellen's to complete the uploading of the PDF file and to finish the design of the book's cover. I know it's going to take at least two hours to do the entire thing because I've never done it before. So I think I'm going to have to wait until this coming Monday, when I will be going over to Ellen's anyway. Also, I've been very busy working on this week's blog, and tending to things that I need to do here at the apartment.

Monday, September 13

I decided to walk over to Ellen's yesterday after work. The air was stifling. I was drenched and fatigued when I got over there. She had iced tea waiting and the laptop on the table. I posted the blog early so that I could devote my time today and through the week to completing the book. Yesterday, I managed to successfully upload it. So at least I got *that* part out of the way! I also worked on the cover with the Cover Wizard. But I wasn't able to focus very well because of my being so utterly depleted.

Ellen wisely suggested that we go get something to eat. We went to Hooligan's, where I had my usual (veggie burger, fries, honey mustard for dipping and Sprite). It was so very good. Ellen then needed to go to a couple of stores. Though I was tired and needed both a shave and a shower, I rode along with her. At Earthfare, I smelled the votive candles (with the patchouli and lavender smelling particularly good) and checked out the hippy chicks. At Rosewood, I got the smoked deviled tofu salad for Wednesday's lunch when I go back to work. When I got home and tried the salad, it was terrible, and I dumped it. Oh, well.

Tuesday, September 14

After doing a load of laundry, Ellen picked me up and we went directly over to her house. I told her that I would need to be on her laptop for at least three hours. I was on it from 6:00pm to 9:30pm, drinking only water and not eating any dinner. I worked on the cover design, the text on the front and back covers, and the pricing for both the trade paperback and the eBook edition. Remarkably, by 9:25pm, I had actually finished the process to publish *Vastness* and had ordered a proof copy to make sure it looks okay! At that point, my ISBN number will be officially added.

Ellen, however, was extremely angry that I had commandeered her laptop for the entire evening, and with some justification, as she had emails to check from the realtor. I reminded her that I had mentioned that I would be working on the MacBook all evening. For some reason, she didn't think that that would be the case. I apologized numerous times, letting her know that I really couldn't stop at the various points because I wanted to get the book finished. But she was angry and barely spoke the rest of the night. I didn't tell her that my book was basically done and ready for publication. There seemed to be no point, given her state of mind. Once again, oh well.

She went to bed (and to sleep) in edgy silence, while I (now with a headache from not eating) sat in the kitchen alone, under a dimmed light, scarfing down Chik'n Tenders with honey mustard, coleslaw, tempeh salad, and organic red grapes. Feelings of regret, bafflement, and gratitude arose and disappeared within me. Alas, Ellen doesn't realize that when I utter practically anything now, particularly "I'm sorry," that it is said from the deepest part of me. All one can do is to say the words and hope that the person fully receives them.

Friday, September 17

I watched a DVD on Mepkin Abbey, a community of Trappist Catholic monks, in (appropriately enough) Monks Corner, South Carolina. These are compassionate and well-meaning men, but nearly all of what they said about spirituality was wrong. For instance, we are not brought closer to God through chastity, poverty or other vows. The closeness is *already* there. For we *are* awareness or presence, which are just other names for God. And you certainly don't require the support of anyone when your understanding is solid and without question.

Even much of what the religious experts and commentators had to say about spirituality was off the mark. If you are drawn to live in such a community, that is perfectly fine. It is indeed a lovely setting, and I would love to visit it on some occasion. But the monastic life is not a necessary avenue to God, who/which is everywhere simultaneously, and lives fully within each of us at this very moment. Whatever names we use--God, Brahman, Jehovah, the lovely-sounding Emmanuel--we are talking about presence/awareness. I could go on and on, of course. Just know that we are talking about a Supreme Reality that is both everlasting and essentially unchanging. Thus names are irrelevant. Only direct experience of that Reality is what is vital.

Monday, September 20

I called FedEx last night. The guy I talked with (very nice and helpful) said that the book arrived three days ago, apparently while I was at work, but they don't know where the package is now! I left my cell phone number for them to reach me, though it may take two or three days for them to find it and then to make a re-delivery, at which time I will again be at work! I wanted to be able to announce the book's publication this week on my blog posting. But it looks like that isn't going to happen. Dang. So I've decided not to publish a new blog this week because I want the next posting to include information about *Vastness*. Also, I need to see the book so I can make sure that it looks okay, and then go to Lulu to add the ISBN number to it, to make the publication official.

Wednesday, September 22

Vastness finally arrived yesterday. It physically looks fine, but there are numerous grammatical and formatting errors in it that I should have taken the time to catch. Still, I went immediately over to Ellen's to have the ISBN placed on the book. The instructions that I had gotten off the Web were not detailed enough, and I wasn't able to complete the processing. I emailed Lulu's customer service and, within minutes, they sent me a clear and easy-to-understand answer. Now the book has an ISBN number and is finally official.

Wednesday, September 29

Well, the new blog is posted, including my announcement of *Vastness*. I wish I could say, "Oh, what a relief it is." But I'm conflicted over the book's formatting errors, sentences that didn't upload properly, and the grammatical errors in sections and pieces that I foolishly added *after* Fiona had proofed the manuscript. She, by the way, clicked on the book's cover on Lulu and loved it. But I'm going to have to do something about the book. For I definitely don't want it read or purchased in that condition!

October

Friday, October 1

I bought a MacBook Pro! Ellen took me to Best Buy, and I pulled out my credit card and bit the bullet. I treated us to breakfast at Panera's while Best Buy installed the software for me. It is such a sexy and beautiful laptop, and I'm *thrilled* to be able to finally have one!

Tuesday, October 12

I haven't written in a while because I've been getting to know my beautiful new Mac. Also, there is the matter of my having second thoughts about publishing the diary. *Vastness* hasn't sold a single copy, which is probably a blessing. For I've become even more bothered by the many flaws in it, flaws that I was too tired to see before and after publication. So I emailed Greg Banks to see if he could make the corrections I wanted on Lulu. I tried to do it myself and managed to make a small mess of things. Greg wrote immediately back and said that he would, and I told him that I would send him a payment. I also sent him the list of things that needed changing. It's still going to take at least two weeks before the changes show up in the book, because Greg is busy with other projects.

Meanwhile, people will be buying the flawed, first edition, instead of the revised one. Oh, how I cringe at that.

Wednesday, October 13

Ellen sold her house today. The closing will be December 6, the day when she absolutely must be out, though she will likely be gone by then. Still, it seems as if we will be having Thanksgiving together, which is great.

Tuesday, October 19

I'm sitting quietly in Barnes & Noble, feeling the benevolent fullness of presence. Being surrounded by all these books and magazines conjures up numerous childhood memories. For not only were there lots of books in my family home, but I practically lived in the libraries in the various schools and colleges that I attended, as well as at the public libraries that were close to me. Nearly all children are made better by reading to them, speaking graciously to them (and in *full* sentences), having books and computers within easy reach and sight, nourishing their interests and proclivities, praising their successes, and giving encouragement and insights into their failures. And, of course, the parent or guardian may broach the topic of them being more than mere bodies and minds, but awareness itself. Such a talk may or may not work, of course. It depends on the temperaments of the children and the clarity of the parents' words.

Thursday, October 28

The DVD player stopped working. I cannot afford to get it fixed. I guess I'll have to watch DVDs on my MacBook Pro. That will be an adjustment, but that is simply the way the situation is right now.

Friday, October 29

I adore the following words that Buddha spoke to an assembly at Vulture's Peak: "I have a subtle teaching of the treasury of the true dharma eye, the wondrous mind of nirvana, the true form of no forms. It does not rely on words and is transmitted outside the scriptures. I give it to Mahakashyapa."

Buddha bestowed his transmission on Mahakashyapa (perhaps his most astute disciple) because he smiled when Buddha twirled a small flower in his hand; no one else in the assembly saw the meaning of Buddha's gesture. Whether Mahakashyapa had a clear and sudden understanding of himself at that point will likely be speculated for eons. Perhaps it was just an intuitive one or simply a significant pause, which Buddha would have to clarify for Mahakashyapa. But some deep insight seems to have occurred, and that lovely moment was captured at that meeting.

Vulture's Peak (a terrific name!) is one of several dramatic rock shelters outside of the ancient city of Rajgir, India. Though vultures did indeed perch on some of its pinnacles, it was Buddha's favorite retreat site. He made many discourses there, and it was also where another of his chief disciples, Sariputta, came to his full understanding. Though

I've never had an inclination to visit spiritual locales, I'd go to Vulture's Peak in a heartbeat, provided it wasn't in the broiling summer. The trip would be not to worship anything or anyone, but to revel in this peaceful, historic, and atypical setting. You can even go into certain caves, such as the Sukarakhata (the Boar's Grotto) where Buddha is said to have delivered the *Discourse of Long Nails* (about life being more than suffering) and the *Sukarakhata Sutta* (where Buddha explains why a monk who did an irreverent act should not be banished from the assembly; for the monk had doubtlessly gone beyond the 'yoke' of the teachings to a final understanding of himself). Vulture's Peak was also where Buddha delivered the *Prajnaparamita Sutras*, which he said contain the true essence of his voluminous teaching.

Saturday, October 30

Greg Banks made the slew of corrections and improvements to *Vastness* for me. And he did them quickly, too. He then offered to format the manuscript for the Kindle Reader, for *half* his normal fee! *Vastness* would at least be on Amazon as an eBook. Though I don't need to spend any more money, I quickly said, "Absolutely!"

November

Monday, November 1

Ellen and I went to Harper's (a nice restaurant in Five Points that focuses on American cuisine) with Beth and Allan, who are long-time friends of ours. Allan is a high school English teacher and Beth works at ETV, the Public Television affiliate here in Columbia. The conversation quickly steered to politics, about which I said hardly a word. I just wasn't interested. I have voted, and I have not voted. My life is my life, and it is not an example for anyone. So I just enjoyed my margarita--which I occasionally order when I go out--as the rest of the gang chatted and debated.

Interestingly, I didn't drink at all for the longest time after this understanding occurred. I've never been a drinker anyway; however, I would occasionally have a margarita, which I love. But after the awakening, I was afraid that the drinking would have some sort of adverse effect on this incredible non-state. It was a foolish notion, of course, but the thought was there. And it wasn't that I *needed* the drink to feel happy. It was more the taste of the margarita, the mix of sweet, salt, and tartness that was appealing here. Now I happily drink and get the inevitable buzz from margaritas whenever I go out to dinner. The buzz appears within this peace and spaciousness. It's just like another thought, feeling, or sensation. And it is witnessed unblinkingly.

Thursday, November 4

The Richland County Public Library (our central, beautiful library for the Midlands area) has ordered a copy of *A Vastness All Around*! I'm delighted, for that will allow people who can't afford to purchase the book the opportunity to read it, if they are so disposed. It's a little strange to do a title search on the library's website and see the title of the book actually come up. Stranger still is to see my name beside it. But again, I'm thrilled.

Wednesday, November 10

Well, I've officially started revising this diary. I should have begun much earlier, for this means that I will be pressed into the same working madness as I was a few months ago, making corrections and revisions *and* going through the publishing routines with Lulu far into next year. But on this book, Fiona and I will be doing multiple rounds of editing and proofing. And that should go somewhat smoothly since she, Greg, and I have a great working relationship, and I'm now more familiar with Lulu's workings. Also, there's the glorious fact that I now have my very own MacBook Pro, which should make the process considerably easier.

Saturday, November 13

The leaves on the trees around the mall are finally starting to change, especially the Callery Pears along the front thruway. My favorite area to view the fall resplendence is the rear of the mall. There, an elegant stand of twenty-year old trees runs along the back-road. The trees range from elms and red maples to flowering dogwoods and sweetgums. The leaves go from orange and light golden (the yellow poplars mostly) to bright red and deep wine (such as the sassafras). Particularly striking is the lone sourwood, which is usually one of the first to turn its vibrant crimson and orange. Directly behind this arboreal expanse runs a shallow polluted stream, and behind the stream stands a jade-wall of kudzu, bamboo plants, coastal plain willows, towering pitch pines, and an occasional palmetto. As the season deepens, I'll park the security truck at various points along the route, so that I can view and protect the property, as well as take in this tranquil autumnal splendor.

Monday, November 15

A Vastness All Around is now available for the Amazon Kindle! Greg Banks did the Byzantine conversion for me, and we both, in tandem, set it up on Amazon, with him doing the more intricate chores. It was his suggestion, saying that at least I could have *Vastness* on Amazon in the Kindle version. Also, I read somewhere that e-Books and Kindle versions can sell thirty per cent more of your titles. I'm just delighted that the book is available to readers who have and love their Kindles.

Thursday, November 18

I receive a beautiful email from a blog reader. It reads, in part:

"A week or so ago, I started reading *No Death, No Fear* (Thich Nhat Hanh), and when I came to the Teaching on Impermanence section, the world stopped. The beauty of beingness and the recognition of intimacy and love were all so clear, so silent. It was clarity without notions or thoughts or anyone at all.

Days later, something arises in me that wants to tell my love-goddess wife Francesca about my insight. And I do, but she doesn't know what I'm trying to say. Then I notice I don't know either! And I no longer even hear what my mouth is trying to say, as I fall into her gaze and just sit in perfect peace. The reality of the moment is upon us, just a witnessing as the infinite expresses itself...this life is so blessed."

Yes, when it comes to love, oftentimes stillness, silence, or even a gaze say more than words ever could. And if your partner happens to have a deep devotion for you too, then he or she fully knows (or at least intuits) what you are expressing in your touch or hushness. Such an unfathomable way of communicating with one another is, of course, one of the many joys of a profound relationship. Indeed, love is one of the closest manifestations of awareness. So when it is felt for a particular person or thing, it is quite singular, even sacred.

Saturday, November 20

A person called who had heard me on the Urban Guru Cafe. She loved the sound of my voice, which I find bland and boring. We had a long and perceptive conversation (at least I *hope* it was insightful). She now lives in Florida, but had previously resided in Virginia. While living in the latter, she was "just beginning to understand there was something else going on, that I was starting to question who and what I actually am. I read in the paper some person called Jiddu Krishnamurti was appearing at the Kennedy Center. It seemed to be a big deal so I got a ticket. Thousands were in attendance. This small man walked onto a huge empty stage to talk about self-realization, and all I remember was him saying, "Why are you asking me?" Believe me, I was vexed-- all this money for a ticket, and he is asking us why we are here? He died a few months later. I still remember the moment and now it makes sense to me. But I am still not 'getting it'...sigh...I'm still asking...I still want another illusion to point out my illusion."

I told her how excellent her points were, particularly the one about wanting one illusion to clarify another. Krishnamurti's remark has some merit: The answer is within you, and you must discern it for yourself. Then again, he was there on stage to be asked questions, and people were in their seats wanting to hear his responses. But I suspect he was simply attempting to be witty. The people that were attuned to him could just as easily have turned their focus upon themselves. Had they done so, some of them just might have suddenly beamed with utter wonder and gratitude, as they remarked, "How could I have missed it for so long?"

Why are there so many satsangs and retreats? Because people who sound and *appear* spiritual come along, and seekers are quickly taken in by their words and demeanor. These people seem to fit the notion of who and what an enlightened person is. The talks and retreats may end up being entertaining, but precious few insights are gleaned from them. Now, this isn't meant to say that such outings are a complete waste of time. There are those rare occasions when they can be both helpful and conducive to self-reflection. And when there is good food, perceptive discussions, and a direct pointing to presence, then such talks and occasions are marvelous indeed.

Sunday, November 21

My insomnia returns. I wake up at 2:00am and can't go back to sleep. At that hour, it's too late to take any sleeping pill, so I get up at 2:20am, get dressed, make coffee, and go straight to the computer. It's really good that I'm not in a live-in relationship. My poor partner would suffer indeed.

Wednesday, November 24

I'm at Barnes & Noble, typing away. Presently, I'm the only person in the cafe. I've just finished reading the December issue of *Vanity Fair*. Lots of good stuff there: A heartfelt and witty interview with Christopher Hitchens, who is suffering from cancer; Aaron Sorkin's work desk (Sorkin is a vibrant and gifted scriptwriter); a James Wolcott piece on National Public Radio (Wolcott is a vigorous wordsmith too, and I generally enjoy his stuff), and a brief but complimentary review of the late Barry Hannah's collections of stories. I knew Barry when he was teaching at Clemson University. We had several long, raucous, and sharp-witted conversations together before the University of Mississippi seduced him away. He was a great language stylist and storyteller. He also loved cigarettes and alcohol, both of which may have contributed to his death at the relatively young age of sixty seven.

I love *Vanity Fair*, but once I've scanned the magazine to see what I want to read, I find it hard to locate the articles again. Even the Table of Contents is scattered and difficult to pinpoint! So I end up saying, "forget it" and, in my inglorious impatience, toss the magazine down, and get back to work. Ditto with people and situations, which is neither bad nor good, but simply the way things are with this particular personality.

Thursday, November 25

Thanksgiving. I worked on the blog and diary here at the apartment until around 10:00am. Then Ellen picked me up, and we went over to her place, where I helped her pack more boxes. We cooked some dishes (I made a pecan pie, and she roasted Brussels sprouts) to take over to Lisa's, her new friend who lives across the street. Lisa invited us over for a holiday dinner there. We also took a tofu turkey from Rosewood Market. My pie didn't turn out well (overcooked), but neither did some of the other dishes. Everyone had a good time, though. Lisa had invited a trio of friends over; one of them was a Chinese graduate student, who just happens to live in my apartment building!

The day was sunny and temperate, with highs in the mid-seventies. I sat in an old, wooden rocker on the cozy porch. The soft autumn light was exquisite as it played upon the remaining leaves on the trees. The ground itself was covered mostly with russet maple fronds, which would occasionally scatter or turn into a whirlwind of sepia flakes whenever a long breeze blew. Everything that appeared seemed imbued with presence, giving it life and augmenting its beauty. So much so, in fact, that I sometimes had to put down the book that I was reading and give full attention to this consummate stillness.

Monday, November 29

A really jam-packed day. After work, I spent the rest of the afternoon and evening doing my least favorite of all things: Going to the DMV (Department of Motor Vehicles) to get my driving license renewed. At the DMV, I sat amidst the multitude of people from a multitude of ethnic groups and social classes. Everyone seemed overly focused in some way: Talking or texting on cell phones, speaking to the strangers about some sort of vehicular legality, or trying to make sense of some form that they had been handed. There was no one just sitting quietly and in the moment. When I sit like that, it's not even 'being in the moment.' It *is* the moment. One could even call it a non-moment of peace and placidity. There is no one 'being' or doing anything. You are alive to the sounds and people around you, but they are appearing *in* presence, that great immenseness. I sat like that, knowing it would probably be a while before I was summoned. But after only five minutes, my ticket number was called. I went up to the attractive DMV employee and quickly paid for the renewal. Then I got my picture taken and the license sealed, all in another five minutes! And even the photograph was a good one. Emaho!

December

Wednesday, December 1

Ellen left this morning. We said goodbye in her Volkswagen after she dropped me back at the apartment last night. She had a sleepless night and a terrible morning, for Teddy--her very strong, feral and intuitive black cat--knew that Ellen was up to something. He fought her tooth and paw, though *never* hurting her, and escaped from the house entirely. Ellen had no choice but to leave, with Midtown and Zoey in their respective cages. Ellen's best childhood friend, Lon, was waiting outside the house to follow her in his SUV, which was loaded to the ceiling with more boxes.

Recollections of her arose last night, as I made a cup of Bellagio French Vanilla Gourmet Hot Chocolate from a pack she gave me last week. As I sipped the delicious brew, I listened to Nat King Cole's *The Christmas Song*, the CD which I always play in the holidays. But this time, the beautiful and classic melody was tinged with sadness and entreaties for wishing Ellen a safe journey to her new, snowy home.

Thursday, December 2

Ellen called me at work several times from her cell phone. Ironically, she called at just or near the time memories of her were coming up. Yes, I'm missing her. But there is no loneliness here. None whatsoever. Just those occasional sentiments, some potent and deep, and this utter benediction for which all words pale.

Sunday, December 5

Ellen left her incredibly comfortable, queen-size bed for me. What a gift! I paid two of the maintenance guys at work to help me get the bed from her former house to my apartment. It feels *so* good, and a bit strange, to have her bed in *my* bedroom. Doubly-strange is sleeping in it without her. Ellen also gave me some of her old sheets, which were soft and marvelously familiar. I left the bedroom light on for a minute or two, as I took it all in. Then I switched the light off and slept very, very well.

Monday, December 6

Ellen also left me a shoe-box full of stuff that was on top of the bed. I'm only now getting to it, since I was so exhausted and busy yesterday. The shoebox includes: My toothbrush, my contact lens case, an unopened bottle of hydrogen peroxide, Target Optical eyeglass cleaner (which I always used on my glasses when I was over there), and my thread-worn but immensely comfortable black bedroom slippers. In one of the slippers, I found some Nature's Gate Organics Mandarin Orange & Patchouli Deodorant. This was Ellen's, but I loved and used it. What a surprise and a delight. I am so greatly moved.

Tuesday, December 7

Worked at the desk until around 9:00am. Then I took the bus to the Original Pancake House for my weekly pecan waffle, scrambled eggs, and grits. Our usual waitress, Kenyatta, rushed over and said that she would have the "coffee and tea coming up." I told her that there would be "only coffee from now on" and explained about Ellen's leaving. She said that she was so sorry, and I said that it was okay, and that I "wished Ellen well." Kenyatta thought this was very "brave" of me to say. But there is no bravery at all. I *do* wish her well!

After eating, I stepped back out into the cold and went next door to Starbucks, where I sat and read Saturday's *New York Times*. I came across an interesting article by Benedict Carey, entitled *Tracing the Spark of Creative Problem-Solving*. In the piece, Carey quotes Marcel Danesi (a professor of anthropology at the University of Toronto and the author of *The Puzzle Instinct: The Meaning of Puzzles in Human Life*) who said of creativity: "It's imagination, it's inference, it's guessing; and much of it is happening subconsciously." Danesi further stated, "It's all about you, using your own mind, without any method or schema, to restore order from chaos."

Yes, that works well for conceptual issues, but not for knowing your natural state. There is no guessing or imagination. Indeed, it is imagination that often gets in the way of the seeing, since seekers readily envision enlightenment or awakening to be something that it is not. Reasoning, however, can certainly play a role in this understanding. For instance, after coming to the clear and logical conclusion that consciousness (which is a state of awakeness, as well as sentience) couldn't possibly be what you are (since, among other things, it constantly changes) you are genuinely paused. In fact, you can be stilled in such a way that presence shines clearly and beautifully before you. You see that you have been looking directly at it and through it during all the time of your searching. Thus, there is a natural and permanent 'shifting' from conceptual conclusions to a living reality.

After Starbucks, I walked past the Fresh Market a few stores down in the beautiful Trenholm Square shopping center. The front of the store was warmly loaded with basket displays, Christmas trees, rosemary trees, and tall baskets of cinnamon brooms, which smelled *so* good! Their sight and aroma always remind me of the holidays, and I always look for them right after Thanksgiving. I went inside and, though waddling in coffee already, tried some of their exquisite Kona Blend. I then ambled through the store with the quietly happy holiday shoppers. The caramel apple walnut pie looked scrumptious, but it was ridiculously expensive. I went to the spice rack and smelled the ground allspice, which is utterly redolent and begs-to-be-purchased (though I resisted). Then it was time to head to the bus stop. But a sudden wave of heartache washed over me. I sat on the bench in front of the store, perplexed but not overly bothered. Festive shoppers bustled by, as melancholy swept over the whole of my being, growing stronger and stronger until it simply disappeared into vastness.

I got up, finally, and hurried to my approaching bus across the highway. Back at the apartment, a load of dirty clothes awaited me. And more work on my blog.

Thursday, December 9

John LeKay, editor of *Enlightenment Magazine*, wants to do another interview with me. This one would center on the publication of *Vastness*. I said, "Sure" before forgetting that I was knee-deep in the writing and editing of the diary. Fortunately, it will take John a few days (or weeks) before he emails the first set of queries (I sent him a PDF copy of the book). So we'll see how it goes.

Monday, December 13

Fiona sent me the February corrections for the diary. I'm thrilled, though I haven't had a chance to even go through the January proofs yet! But I'm glad she's moving along. She's like that: Once she starts a project, she finishes it. Indeed, she and I are the same in that regard. Perhaps that's one of the reasons we work so well together. And I love how she broaches the issue of something being semi-provocative or simply not making sense: "Sweetie, I was wondering if this passage might be a tad much."

Yesterday was windy, chilly, and rainy. Today, it's supposed to be sunny, but with a high of only

38°F. The dawn frigidness certainly indicates that projection. I make my usual peanut-butter-and-strawberry-jam sandwich on soft, whole wheat bread, while having the most penetrating thoughts that one can imagine--thoughts and phrases pointing to that which *cannot* be imagined! This is what the 'awakened' life is all about: The mix of the ordinary and the profound. Practically anyone can have this life, if he or she takes a moment to discern the fullness of our seemingly ordinary, everyday awareness. And truly, nothing could be simpler.

Tuesday, December 14

This morning, I walked to Barnes & Noble with my laptop and went over Fiona's January corrections and suggestions. Her changes and advice were so helpful and astute. Because there was a lot of prose to get through in the January entries, I stayed until 2:00pm, for I wanted to get through the entire month. When I walked back to the apartment, it seemed even colder than it did earlier this morning, when the temperature was in the mid-30s. It had only gotten up to 37° or 38°, but the wind was blowing steadily, making it feel like it was 30°! There was the oddly nice mix of my covered body and hands still feeling the cold, and this spaciousness which the frigidity could not touch. Yet, the body was certainly making it feelings heard: "You idiot, I'm freezing out here! Why didn't you wear more clothes!?" This is what the body does beautifully: Focuses on its survival.

Thursday, December 16

A work of genius--whether in fiction, non-fiction, art, spirituality, music, or anything else--has the following characteristics: It is distinctive (it stands out in some engaging and captivating way); it is elegant (though it may appear abstract, dissonant, or even simple); it is difficult to imagine being without (Google, Mac computers, Bach's music, Glenn Gould's renditions of Bach's music); it possesses unending richness (Shakespeare's plays, Zen masters' brush calligraphy, Rodin's sculptures, Sarah Vaughn's singing, Marian Macpartland's jazz compositions, Swami Nikhilananda's translation of the *Mandukya Upanishad*); and, finally, it gives you pause.

Sunday, December 19

My friend Peter is back in Switzerland, and he sent me five gorgeous and idyllic pictures of mountain-side chalets with snow up to their roofs. And on the roofs themselves, there were a couple of feet of even more snow! In addition to being in Switzerland, Peter has purchased a copy of *A Vastness All Around*, which, he says, he is thoroughly enjoying. Ah, a holiday greetings card with snowy pictures from my dear email-friend...What a treat!

Monday, December 20

Ellen is flying back to Columbia this afternoon, and I'm taking the last of my sick days today so that I can help her try to capture Teddy and then drive with her back to Columbus. It will be a thirteen hour trip, much of it in bitter cold and snow. But I want to be there for Ellen on this. I've spent the morning packing and preparing to take stuff on a plane (she's paying for my ticket back). I haven't flown in eight years, so I'm not sure what and what not to take. The plan is for Ellen to fly here, rent a car, drive over to her former house, go into the back yard, and call Teddy. She is going to take some salmon, his favorite food. The traps that some of her girl friends have left for Teddy haven't worked, for he's far too savvy for that.

At first, Ellen was going to take him to her vet, get him checked out, and board him there overnight. She would then stay here with me, and we would get an early start the next morning. Now she thinks it would be better to capture Teddy, get immediately on the road, and stop at a pet-friendly Red Roof inn somewhere on the other side of Charlotte, North Carolina. That sounds like a good plan to me, too. So we are going to give it a go, if she actually gets him.

She called me last night to thank me, once again, for being "willing to do all of this, and without a single complaint." I told her that one of the hallmarks of our friendship is the help that we forthrightly give to one another. She chuckled and said that's why I probably wouldn't have to worry about her finding a new man in Columbus: "What guy would do that for a girlfriend, much less for a cat!" But I want Teddy safe and happy too. The same with Ellen also, whether she is with "another man or some hot, ravenous, middle-aged woman."

She roared (and she hadn't laughed in a while) and finally uttered, "Oh yeah. You would *really* be okay with that, wouldn't you, especially if you could come up to visit!?"

Wednesday, December 22

It's 6:00pm and Ellen just left, having successfully managed to capture Teddy, after trying to get him for three days. She arrived on Monday afternoon, and stayed here during the two nights. During the morning and afternoon, she went over to her old house (which was strange and sad for her to see, with its new owner there) to try to find Teddy and get him into the carrier.

Otherwise, Ellen and I had a great time together. It was so nice to sleep with her, of course, and in her glorious bed once again! We also were able to do some of the same things we always did on holidays, such as going to the Fresh Market, having a cozy meal at Rosewood Market (where I stocked up on vegetarian chili boxes), grocery shopping at Publix, and going to the Dollar Store, where I bought Christmas presents for myself: Yellow Post-It notes, batteries, crazy glue, light bulbs (we nondual writers gotta have illumination), a cookie pan, shaving cream, dish detergent, and Dermasil lotion (we writers gotta have soft, smooth, irresistible skin). We also had some great meals right here in the apartment. I moved the printer off the dinner table. It and the iMac have been there since I first moved here. It was great to actually be able to sit face-to-face, while enjoying our food. It was *so* nice, in fact, that the printer (which no longer works anyway) has been placed in the storage closet. Two bamboo place-mats that Ellen gave me are now on the table, and they are where I now will be having my meals, instead of on a plastic dinner tray while sitting on the sofa.

Feelings of missing my long-time partner come up as I unpack my clothes for the now-cancelled plane trip. I make cinnamon muffins for the week and work on the blog. Periodically, I wish her and Teddy safe travels on their long and snowy way home.

Saturday, December 25

Ellen called last night, with the words, "Merry Pre-Christmas!" We laughed and then talked for over forty five minutes. She has one of those Virtual Calling cards where your long distance charges are just a few pennies each minute. She told me that she would be driving down to Cincinnati to spend Christmas day (today) with her family there. It was cold, she said; in the 20°s and with snow flurries, but the roads were clear.

I worked on the blog and the diary, answered email, and watched DVDs (the rest of *30 Rock: Season Four* and *Vanilla Sky* with Tom Cruise). Since it was the holidays, I went to Kroger yesterday and treated myself to affordable and delicious items, including a large, frozen vegetable lasagna, Chik'N Patties (that I dipped into honey mustard), and Southern potato salad. For dessert, I cooked a large, frozen apple pie, which I enjoyed with fat-free vanilla ice cream.

It would be great to do some 'Christmassy' things with friends. But I have none. When I'm in a relationship, the woman *is* my friend. So I've never made it a point to cultivate friendships. But now, perhaps, I should think about doing that, if only for the practicalities of life ("Hey Pal-of-Mine, my refrigerator's bare! Could I hitch a ride to the store?") But this Christmas, I am very much alone, and it's strange indeed.

Sunday, December 26

It's 4:00am, and it's snowing! It's so heavy and beautiful, as it floats out of the night sky. Alas, I have to go into work today. I'm also Officer in Charge. I'm sure it will be a busy day if the mall opens this morning, and I'm pretty certain it will, given that this is a big shopping day. But the mall being opened is not my call. That's management's decision. So we'll see. For now, I'm enjoying my coffee and working on this week's blog, which goes up tomorrow.

Now it's 3:30pm, and I'm back from work. It was busy. The Maintenance/Operations manager--a super nice guy--decided not to come in and told me to use my own judgment on things (after making sure that a slew of things were properly done). Some snow is remaining on the ground, but not much. After showering, I stretch out on the sofa and think of which books I'm going to order from Amazon as a belated Christmas present to myself. And I quickly decide upon Derek Walcott's new poetry collection *White Egrets* and Mahesh Bhatt's *A Taste of Life: The Last Days of U. G. Krishnamurti*. Getting those grand-sounding titles starts me thinking about the fact that the more original a person is, the more difficult it is to write about his or her life. Mahesh has wisely selected to concentrate just on U. G.'s final years. A grand biography would have been fine, but it would have been a glorious failure. Why? Because with those who are awakened, there is always a substantial part of the person's existence that the biographer simply can't capture. Even to write a biography of such a brilliant writer as Walcott would probably fail to capture him satisfactorily. Ditto any expansive biography of such geniuses as Nat King Cole, Glenn Gould, Emily Dickinson, Huang Po, and Siddhartha Gautama (the Buddha).

Monday, December 27

Happy Birthday, Big Guy! And no, I honestly don't know how old I am. I'd have to add it up, which I simply am not interested in doing. There is no escapism here. It just isn't of overwhelming interest to me. I know I'm in my late fifties. That's close enough, and it's something to tell people if they ask and still appear to be sane. I know the year I was born, of course, and could do the math. But age is really such a non-issue for me. And it's really not a factor when it comes to self-knowledge.

Still, I think I qualify as a late bloomer, which is perfectly fine. Buddha didn't awaken until he was thirty-five, and he taught for the next forty-five years, before he died. U.G. Krishnamurti didn't come to his solid understanding until he was fifty years old. And Joshu--perhaps my favorite Zen monk--didn't begin the study of Zen until he was sixty, became self-realized at eighty, and instructed until (it is said) he was one hundred and twenty!

Further, Kenneth Clark called the period of filming *Civilisation*--the television series he began working on when he was sixty-four--"the happiest years of his life." And John Russell, writing in the *New York Times*, noted that when the Dutch American abstract expressionist Willem de Kooning was in his seventies, he was "still inventing new ways of mixing the paint, new ways of getting it to do his will, new ways to accommodate the thrusts of the psyche." In the early 1980s, when de Kooning was eighty years old and ailing with poor eyesight and dementia, he still produced, said Russell, "The simplest and most shimmering paintings of his career...the emptied-out white of the background predominated, as did the exhilarating sense of forms caught in mid-dance." Even the debilitated painter himself recognized this and uttered, "I'm becoming freer." What a great thing to have happen: To become "freer."

Tuesday, December 28

Jan Posey, the organizer for the Festival of Healing and Spiritual Awareness, (which is held four times a year in South Carolina, twice in Greenville and twice here in Columbia), wants me to give a talk at the

January 22, 2011 event. I said, "Sure." The Festival has everything from holistic practitioners and natural healing products to intuitive counselors and spiritual writers, which is where I come in. She's given me the noon slot on Sunday, which is one of the "choice times," she said. I thanked her, for I like that slot myself. I'll have to switch one of my work days, but that's no problem. The Festival is a three-day event, beginning that Friday.

Wednesday, December 29

I made cinnamon muffins today, and then went to B & N to work there on my MacBook and read a couple of magazines. A guy I know came over and gave me his *New York Times* that he had finished. Yea! I went back to the apartment, had lunch (peanut-butter and strawberry jam, of course), then went to the clubhouse to look at the big screen TV and see what was happening in the world and weather-wise. There is an evangelical program that I sometimes watch on the afternoons when I'm off. Nobody knows about it. And when anyone walks through, I turn the sound *way* down. For few would understand why I'm watching this particular preacher. No, I am obviously not a Christian, but it's completely okay to be one. He and I probably have opposite views on every major social, religious, and spiritual issue. But I love his delivery, phrasing, and power. And every once and a while, this acclaimed Protestant preacher will say something that is, quite literally, Gospel; when he affirms, for instance, Luke 16:21, "The kingdom of God is within you." How lovely, that. For it is saying that this eternal and measureless province is not something that is attained or that is within our "midst." It is declaring, in no uncertain terms, that your true essence is That! The Kingdom is not merely yours; it is You--immaculate awareness.

Friday, December 31

I found a beautiful religious/spiritual magazine online today. After checking out its archives, I came across a razor-sharp photo of a bearded man meditating on a rock in the middle of a powerful torrent of water. The picture is so crisp and colorful that it reminded me of those 3D View Master transparencies that I reveled in when I was young. The caption read, "Turning inward: A sadhu sits in silence at the frigid headwaters of the Ganga...striving to transcend the thinking mind."

After a moment, I roared with laughter. For this is precisely what spirituality is all about for 99.99 per cent of the world's seekers. And here's the thing: Not only will such practices and endeavors not aid you in stopping your mind (which is just the arising of a thought or image), they will absolutely not help you to discover who and what you are. Why not? Because, among other things, there is this presumed "sadhu" who is "striving" to "transcend the thinking mind." You have already transcended the mind! You are awareness itself! The mind (which is nothing but the periodic appearance of thoughts, emotions, and personality traits) arises *in* you, who are nothing but presence. The photo is clichéd, mythical, sad, and overly-dramatic. Further, it's foolish. For who sits on a rock in the middle of a rushing river in Siberian-like temperatures, wearing merely a gossamer orange-red robe? Alas, only a seeker.

January 2011

Saturday, January 1

Well, the diary is finished. I'm tempted to say that I've come full circle. But there was no journey here, though I'm a full year older, have switched from French Vanilla Creamer to Vanilla Caramel Creamer, and have finally published my first book. Also, I have separated from my partner of many years, though our friendship has deepened considerably over these past twelve months. But these are all incidental arisings in awareness, whose felt-presence has *not* changed in the least.

Fiona sent me a lovely Happy New Year e-card of a black guy named Ronnie playing a Botswana music guitar. The YouTube video shows a dark-complexioned young street musician conferring glassy grins and gazes to an obviously captivated film crew. His strumming is completely natural. He effortlessly plays numerous riffs on the song's beautiful and beguiling melody, making each improvisation seem both new and the same. And that is precisely what has been going on here over the past three-hundred-plus days. No matter what riff or variation I have made on and about nonduality, I have always been pointing to the exact same thing. The song has never varied. It is a song without beginning or end, and it carols within you at this very moment. Listen carefully, and hear it for yourself.

Made in the USA
Columbia, SC
04 April 2019